D0455793

LOCKED IN ICE

LOCKED IN ICE

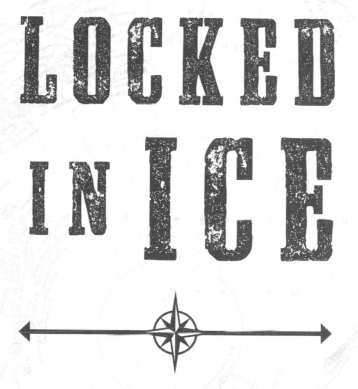

Nansen's Daring Quest
for the North Pole

PETER LOURIE

Christy Ottaviano Books
HENRY HOLT AND COMPANY
NEW YORK

There are many people I'd like to thank for help researching and writing this book. First, a special thank-you to Larry Rosler and Geoff Carroll, longtime friends and wise counselors. Also a big thank-you to the following: Anne Melgård, Guro Tangvald, and Jens Petter Kollhøj at the National Library of Norway in Oslo; Harald Dag Jølle of the Norwegian Polar Institute, in Tromsø; Karen Blaauw Helle, emeritus professor of physiology, Department of Biomedicine, University of Bergen, Bergen, Norway; Carl Emil Vogt, University of Oslo and the Center for Studies of Holocaust and Religious Minorities; Susan Barr, senior polar adviser, Riksantikvaren/Directorate for Cultural Heritage; Dr. Robert Marc Friedman, professor of history, Department of Archaeology, Conservation, and History, University of Oslo; Karin Berg, former director of Oslo's Holmenkollen Ski Museum; Geir O. Kløver, director, *Fram* Museum; Tom Nickelsen Gram, tour guide at the *Fram* Museum; Ola Just Haugbo, manager of information systems, Fridtjof Nansen Institute; Claes Lykke Ragner, head of administration and information, Fridtjof Nansen Institute; Will Ambrose, vice-dean for the School of the Coastal Environment at Coastal Carolina University; and Joanne Muratori. Also Paul Schurke, Gerald Johnson, Charles Johnson, Ed Blechner, Martin Wik Fowler, Maartje Nelemans, Ratchanee and Tor-Inge Eriksen, Atle Larssen, Charlotte Schippers, Samantha and Matt Freemont-Smith, Henry Jova, Kyla and Clifford Hart, Bjorn Peterson, Jessica Anderson, Lindsay Wagner, Erin Schell, and wise counselor Brooke Bessesen. A special thank-you to my editor, Christy Ottaviano, whose unwavering explorer's heart has supported me every step of the way on this Arctic journey.

Henry Holt and Company, *Publishers since 1866*
Henry Holt® is a registered trademark of Macmillan Publishing Group, LLC.
175 Fifth Avenue, New York, NY 10010
mackids.com

Copyright © 2019 by Peter Lourie
All rights reserved.

Library of Congress Cataloging-in-Publication Data is available.
ISBN 978-1-250-13764-7

Our books may be purchased in bulk for promotional, educational, or business use. Please contact your local bookseller or the Macmillan Corporate and Premium Sales Department at (800) 221-7945 ext. 5442 or by email at MacmillanSpecialMarkets@macmillan.com.

First edition, 2019 / Designed by Erin Schell

Printed in the United States of America by LSC Communications, Harrisonburg, Virginia

10 9 8 7 6 5 4 3 2 1

For Dan Brayton,
whose enthusiasm for all things *Fram* and the sea,
and whose advice and friendship, inspired this book

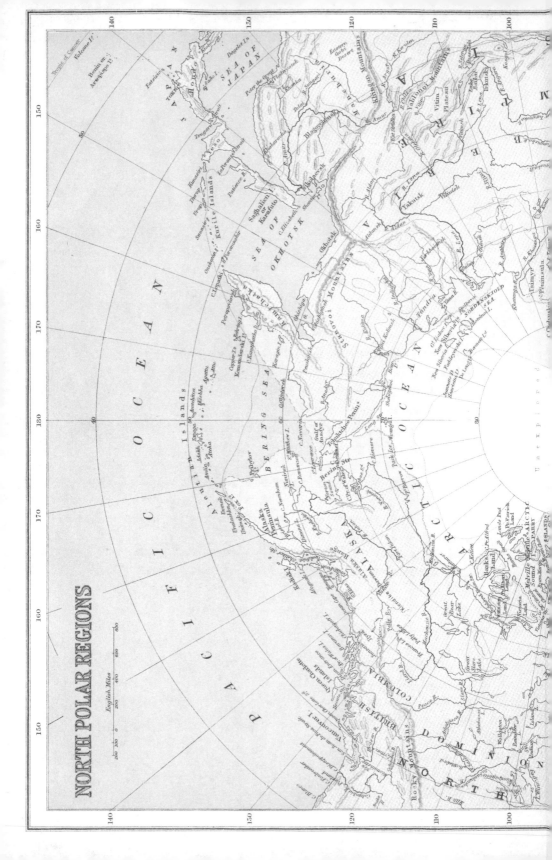

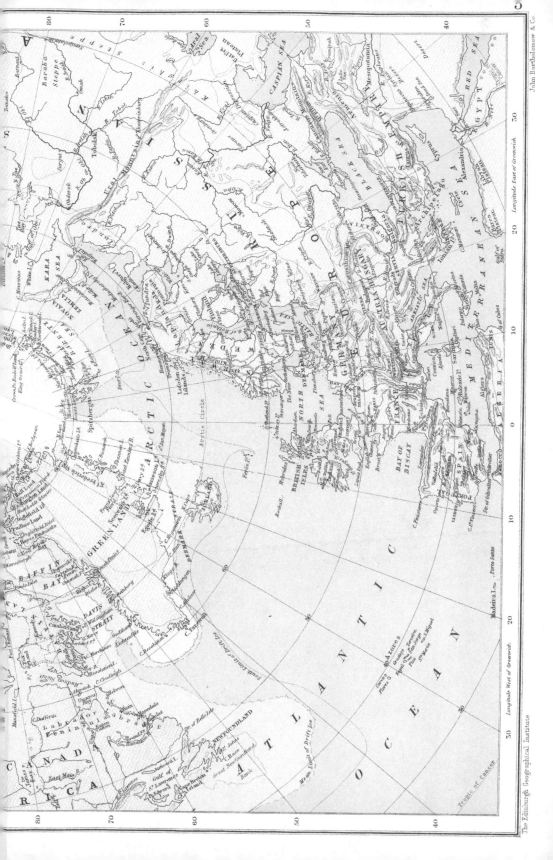

John Bartholomew & Co.

Contents

~ Part One ~
FRIDTJOF NANSEN AND HIS DREAM
1861–1893

~ Part Two ~
THE JOURNEY NORTH
JUNE 24, 1893–MARCH 14, 1894

Part Three
OUTFITTING FOR A TWO-MAN DASH
FEBRUARY 1895

Part Four
ONTO THE ICE
MARCH 14–APRIL 6, 1895

Part Five
TURNING SOUTH
APRIL 8–MAY 31, 1895

Part Six

TO THE KAYAKS
JUNE 1–JULY 22, 1895

Part Seven

LAND AT LAST
JULY 25–AUGUST 15, 1895

Part Eight

FRANZ JOSEF LAND
BEARS, WALRUS, AND A WINTER HOME
AUGUST 16- SEPTEMBER 30, 1895

Part Nine

POLAR NIGHT
OCTOBER 1–DECEMBER 31, 1895

Part Ten

PREPARING TO MOVE AGAIN
JANUARY 1–MAY 18, 1896

Part Eleven

THE JOURNEY SOUTHWARD
MAY 19–JUNE 16, 1896

~ Part Twelve ~

RESCUE
CAPE FLORA, NORTHBROOK ISLAND
JUNE 17, 1896

~ Part Thirteen ~

NORWAY
JUNE 18–AUGUST 12, 1896

~ Part Fourteen ~

HOME
AUGUST 13–SEPTEMBER 9, 1896

Our object is to investigate the great unknown region that
surrounds the Pole, and these investigations will be equally important
from a scientific point of view whether the expedition passes over
the polar point itself or at some distance from it.

—Fridtjof Nansen

The difficult is what takes a little time;
the impossible is what takes a little longer.

—Fridtjof Nansen

The Fram *packed in ice, nighttime, 1895.*

Introduction

*F*RIDTJOF NANSEN, a Norwegian scientist and explorer, had a wild idea. On June 24, 1893, he set sail to explore the Arctic and become the first to reach the North Pole. Others who attempted the same journey met with disaster, often fatal. But Nansen planned to get there by an unusual method. With a crew of twelve and a specially designed ship called the *Fram*, he planned to purposely lock his vessel into the frozen wasteland and "float" on the Arctic pack ice right over the top of the world and down the other side. Veterans of polar expeditions thought he was mad.

In the late nineteenth century, the North Pole was cloaked in mystery. No one had reached the northernmost place on the globe. People wondered if it might be a landmass covered with ice. Or perhaps an open ocean? Did the Arctic hold, as some believed, a lost civilization?

In September 1893, heading into the unknown, Nansen drove his ship into the ice floes of the Arctic Ocean above Siberia, the same ice that had crushed so many vessels in the past. He let powerful polar currents carry the *Fram* slowly northward toward the pole. Then after a year and a half of drifting a few miles a day, icebound and frustrated by the snail's pace of being locked in ice, Nansen realized the ship might miss the North Pole by hundreds of miles. So he made a fateful decision: he and crew member Frederik Hjalmar Johansen would abandon the safety of the ship and cross the polar ice together with three sleds, twenty-eight sled dogs, and two small, canvas-covered kayaks. In the polar spring of 1895, they set off to do what no one on earth had done before—reach the top of the world.

Fridtjof Nansen and Frederik Hjalmar Johansen lifting a sledge over rough ice.

Nansen and Johansen depart on their dash toward the North Pole, 14 March, 1895.
Nansen, second from left; Johansen, second from right.

Within a month, the ice became an impassable jumble of frozen slabs and slushy open water. A mere 232 nautical miles from their destination—and the farthest north any human had ever traveled—the men were forced to turn south in search of land. Aiming for a small group of islands three hundred miles away, they began the harrowing adventure of fourteen months racing the shrinking pack ice and trying to stay alive in an Arctic wasteland. This is their story.

Part One

FRIDTJOF NANSEN
and HIS DREAM

1861–1893

YOUNG SKIER

⟶

*B*ORN IN 1861, Fridtjof (*fritch-off*) Nansen grew up in a privileged family. Nansen's father was a respected lawyer. He was strict and cautious. Not an athletic man, he was slight, unlike Nansen's mother, who was robust and fierce. Despite the social customs of the day, which discouraged women from skiing in public, Nansen's mother skied in trousers. She inspired him with a love of adventure, while his father taught him discipline.

Growing up among the spruce forests, marshes, lakes, and mountains that surround Kristiania (the capital of Norway, later named Oslo), Nansen loved the outdoors. He loved making bows and arrows. An older half brother taught him how to fish, hunt, and survive in the wilderness. Nansen was particularly good at individual sports: swimming, skating, and skiing, especially ski-jumping. He loved winter most. When he was just two, a seven-year-old neighbor taught him to ski, and from the ages of six to eighteen, Nansen skied two miles from his farm to school, and back again.

Clockwise from left:
Attorney Baldur Fridtjof Nansen with his infant son, Fridtjof.
Young Fridtjof Nansen.
Nansen with skis.

Portrait of Nansen as a student.

At fifteen, Nansen won a three-mile speed skating race and did well in ski-jumping and cross-country events. Physically a bit awkward and overweight when he was young, in his late teens he grew slim and muscular. By the time he went to the university in Kristiania, Nansen could walk into a room, and everyone—especially the ladies—would notice him. With striking deep blue eyes and a full head of blond hair, he had a distinct magnetism.

The VIKING *and* FIRST ARCTIC ICE

WHEN NANSEN PREPARED for university, he could not decide which course of study to follow. He wanted to be an engineer, then a soldier, then a forester. To live a life in the open air finally influenced his decision to choose zoology, specifically the study of lower marine creatures of the Arctic Ocean. In zoology, his passion for the natural world combined perfectly with his curiosity and love of science.

Nansen fell in love with the Arctic when he was twenty years old and saw pack ice for the first time. He sailed aboard a sealing vessel called the *Viking* for five adventurous months in the oceans between Spitsbergen, Greenland, and Iceland.

Though he grew up in the forests not far from the sea, this was the first time Nansen learned about ships, and it was his first experience facing a big storm at sea. A few days into the trip, he conquered his seasickness and crossed the Arctic Circle. He listened avidly to the stories of the sailors, who lived like free spirits. He was impressed by their "smiling, reckless courage amid the storm and raging seas."

When ice was spotted at 68° north latitude, Nansen came on deck and peered into the darkness. (For more on latitude and longitude, see glossary.)

Nansen's watercolor sketch: At Sunset, 22nd September, 1893.

"Something white emerged from the blackness," he wrote when he saw the ice. "It grew larger and larger, and gleamed still more white against a background black as night." It was the beginning of the pack ice that stretched for hundreds of miles northward into "the polar night beneath the stars and the northern lights."

Nansen felt a shiver. He'd seen ice before, but nothing compared to this. Here was ice on the "threshold of a new and unknown world." He heard the ice floes colliding, like the roar of great waterfalls. And the sound was thrilling.

Midnight sun over the Arctic.

Drawing the gleaming ice in his sketchbook, he wanted to capture the patterns of light in the polar sky. Nansen learned you could read the ice by studying the sky on the horizon. When ice lies ahead, the clouds on the horizon reflect a white glare, but when there are dark streaks on the underside of low clouds, there will be open water ahead because it is ice-free, a condition called "water sky."

Aboard the *Viking*, Nansen captured birds and dissected them. Through the ice, he took temperatures of the water at various depths and collected water samples, along with small marine animals in his nets. He examined these through a microscope on board and described what he saw. Nansen studied in his cabin for days, but when he emerged, the crew was impressed that he was willing to help them search and hunt for seals. They admired Nansen's excellent marksmanship.

Watercolor of Axel Krefting, captain of the Viking, *and Fridtjof Nansen next to a polar bear that has been shot, 1882.*

Nansen felled his first polar bear on that trip and regretted how easy it was to kill such a magnificent creature: "It seemed so unfair that a little bit of lead should suddenly bring to an end that free life on the boundless expanse of ice."

All spring and early summer, they searched for seal herds, until, like so many unfortunate ships in the Arctic, the *Viking* got frozen into the ice off Greenland. Nansen climbed into the crow's nest and gazed for hours at the unexplored mountains and glaciers on the east coast of Greenland, only a few miles away. He longed to walk out on the ice and go ashore to explore, but the captain would not let him.

After drifting north along the Greenland coast, the ship broke free of the ice in mid-July. By August, Nansen returned to Kristiania with his collection of zoological specimens and a new plan to return to Greenland.

BERGEN *and a* DARING TREK OVER *the* MOUNTAINS

*I*NSTEAD OF RESUMING his studies at the university in Kristiania, however, Nansen took a job as a junior curator at the Bergen Museum. Just shy of his twenty-first birthday, he went to live in a different kind of city than the one he knew. On the west coast of Norway, in the rainy, milder weather of Bergen, Norway's second largest city, Nansen threw himself into

Polar researcher Fridtjof Nansen.

museum work, labeling and studying specimens, learning to draw, teaching himself zoology, and working alongside the famous natural

scientists of his day. He took a particular interest in the structure of the central nervous system of lower marine creatures. Because of new and improved microscopes, scientists of that time were beginning to study the cells of animals. Nansen focused on nerve cells.

Nansen using the microscope at the Bergen Museum, 1882–1888.

After long hours of study in the lab in the gray, wet, sea town, where the sun was forever blocked by clouds, Nansen longed for the crisp snows and spruce forests of his youth. He yearned to be skiing again.

So one day Nansen decided to travel home to enter a ski race back in Kristiania and to visit a girlfriend. He would travel by train, horse carriage, and boat, but mostly he would have to ski through rugged mountainous terrain to get back home. His friends

Fridtjof Nansen postcard.

tried to talk him out of it, but Nansen set out anyway with his heavy wood skis and a hunting dog named Flink ("Clever" in Norwegian) on a 186-mile trek in the dead of winter, mostly across uninhabited, craggy mountains—a trip never attempted before. For days no one knew where he was or whether he was dead or alive.

Along the way, Nansen occasionally met farmers and hunters, but he preferred being alone in the silent wilderness. He was happy skiing on "those wonderful, long, steep mountainsides, where the snow lies soft as eiderdown, where one can ski as fast as one desires. . . . The snow sprays knee-high to swirl up in white clouds behind; but ahead all is clear. You cleave the snow like an arrow. . . ."

When he got to Kristiania, he came in ninth out of fifty-three competitors in the ski jump. He spent ten days in the city, visited his girlfriend, then skied with his dog by his side back through the mountains to Bergen. It gave him a lot of time to think about a Greenland adventure.

GREENLAND

*J*UST ABOUT EVERYONE thought Nansen's idea of skiing across Greenland from the uninhabited east coast to the sparsely populated west would end in disaster. Again, friends tried to dissuade him. Ridiculed in the press in Norway and England, he bucked the tide of popular opinion. Some said that it was stubborn pride that made Nansen willing to risk his own life and the life of his men just to prove his point. But Nansen was sure he would be successful; he would thoroughly plan his trip.

Members of the Greenland expedition breaking camp.

He did, however, have a hard time raising money for the expedition. Yet with typical visionary spirit and iron will, he persisted until a wealthy backer from Denmark finally got behind the project.

Nansen chose an experienced sea captain as his main partner. Five years older than Nansen, red-bearded Otto Sverdrup was tall and mature and already a veteran sea captain at thirty-two. Along with two other hardy Norwegians, all expert skiers, Nansen invited two native Sami men from the north of Norway. Indigenous people, formerly known as Lapps or Laplanders, the Sami live in the far north of Scandinavia and Russia.

Members of the Greenland expedition with Inuit kayaks on the shore of Greenland.

From left to right: *Ole Nilsen Ravna, Samuel Balto, Fridtjof Nansen, Otto Sverdrup, Oluf Christian Dietrichson, and Kristian Kristiansen.*

He tested his expedition equipment in the mountains around Bergen while he finished his research for his doctoral thesis. Everything had to be meticulously thought out. A mistake could be fatal. Nansen decided against taking dogs on the trek because they would require extra food rations, which he and his men could not carry. The expedition would have to travel as light as possible for the one-way trek across the ice cap. Other failed attempts had originated on the west coast, which meant they had had to carry enough food to cross the big island, and then return to where they had started. Nansen was going only in one direction.

Studio-posed photo of Fridtjof Nansen and Otto Sverdrup towing a sledge.

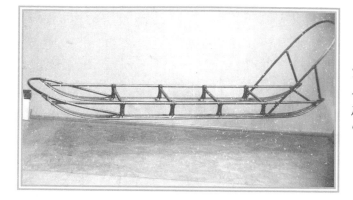

The sledge Nansen designed for the Greenland expedition.

He knew the sleds used by explorers on previous Arctic expeditions were overly burdensome and quickly got bogged down in snow and ice. Always the inventor, Nansen designed five lighter sleds made of ash, which did not require metal nails. They were 9.5 feet long and 1.5 feet wide and weighed only 28 pounds. (The model for this sled, still used today, is called a Nansen sled.) He tested a three-man sleeping bag, a special tent, and a small alcohol camp stove that could warm food while also melting snow for drinking water. Nansen invented a special flask the skiers would fill with snow in the morning and tuck next to their bodies, turning the snow into drinking water while traveling during the day. He designed special clothes and boots and goggles for protection against ice and sun glare.

Nansen planned to eat energy-rich expedition foods—liver pâté, jam, condensed soup and milk, coffee, sugar, and a concentrated, nutritious mixture called pemmican. It was made of ground-up meat mixed with an equal amount of fat, often with the addition of dried berries, and formed into solid cakes. As it turned out, however, because of an error in adding fat to the pemmican compound, the expeditioners on the Greenland trip suffered from acute fat deficiency. Nansen would correct this on his next polar journey.

Nansen also invented something called meat-chocolate, a nutrition-rich mixture of meat powder and chocolate. The sugar from the chocolate, combined with the protein of the meat, gave the men the maximum in calories and energy.

Just as important, Nansen brought scientific instruments, as well as guns, ammunition, cameras, watches, tools, tarps, skis, ski poles, rope, matches, and notebooks. He thought of everything, right down to the sewing needles.

While busily preparing for Greenland, Nansen was able to complete the examinations, lectures, and defense of his research thesis for a doctoral degree in neuroscience (the study of the nervous system and the brain) just before he departed. His research presented a revolutionary idea: that the brain consists of individual, separate nerve cells. To this day, some scientists declare that Nansen's early work on nerve cells is worthy of the Nobel Prize in medicine.

Nansen and his five companions left from Scotland on May 9, 1888, boarding a steamer for Iceland, then took another vessel to Greenland. When the men reached Greenland's east coast in mid-July, they immediately ran into trouble with shifting ice floes and had to camp on the ice for weeks. It was too dangerous to make the final push to shore.

The boats are finally dragged onto land, marking the beginning of the skiing portion of the expedition.

Water crashed at the edge of the ice where they camped; the floes disintegrated beneath them. They drifted far south of where Nansen wanted to begin his trek, and the currents kept jamming ice onto ice. They moved camp to stay alive, and they hardly slept for twelve days. When the team finally reached shore, they returned to their boats, found narrow channels, and rowed northward for days with very little sleep.

The journey through the inland ice.

It took twenty-four days before Nansen's team was ready to make the crossing. They would have to move fast, as the short Arctic summer was already ending. A thick mist lifted in the morning, and the men rose to a sunlit day. With harnesses around their chests, the six men began to haul the sleds over bare rock and rough ice, climbing into uncharted mountains to reach the interior ice cap.

In snow squalls, they climbed to nearly 9,000 feet, dragging their loads across dangerous cracks in the ice called crevasses. They endured temperatures that dropped to −46° Celsius, or −51° Fahrenheit (Nansen used Celsius or centigrade—"C"—which is what scientists use today). They marched for weeks, always hungry and bent over double, either in blinding snow or scorching sunlight. This late in the summer, the snow was like sand, dry and loose, and terrible for skis and the four sleds carrying two hundred pounds each. The fifth sled dragged five hundred pounds and was pulled by Sverdrup and Nansen together. Nansen and his men tried to slake their constant thirst. In camp, they discovered eating straight butter helped. On the trail, to keep their mouths moist, they chewed slivers of bamboo and bits of their wood snowshoes.

When they finally reached the west coast, with its steep and rugged mountains, they were forced to return to the water. On one of the fjords (a fjord is a long, narrow, deep inlet of the sea between high cliffs), Sverdrup built a boat from pieces of their wood sleds and nearby willow trees. After rowing north for days, they glided into the small village of Godthåb. It had taken them forty-nine days, and they had not changed their clothes or washed their faces the whole trip.

Fridtjof Nansen and his five teammates had succeeded in being the first ever to cross the Greenland ice cap. Along the way, they had collected valuable meteorological data, recording temperatures, wind speeds, altitudes, snow depths, and other scientific information about the unexplored interior of Greenland.

Unfortunately, the team missed the last boat sailing for Europe that winter, so the men had to wait seven months for the next ship to take them home. During the dark Arctic winter, Nansen took the opportunity to make friends with the Inuit villagers and learn all he could from them. He learned to speak some of their language.

Inuit family inside their home.

For weeks he lived in their sod-and-stone houses, which were half buried in the ground to preserve warmth through the brutal cold. He learned how to hunt seals with harpoons and how to handle Inuit kayaks made of sealskins. Nansen marveled at how the Arctic people had adapted to such a harsh environment. He even foresaw that the approach of Western society would soon threaten their native way of life. Later he wrote a book about his Greenland experience called *Eskimo Life*.

Pen-and-ink drawing by A. Bloch of an Inuit paddling a kayak in heavy seas.

On the docks of Kristiania, when Nansen finally returned home in 1889, a third of the city's population—as many as forty thousand spectators—came out to cheer their new hero.

Left: Greenland expedition members traveling aboard the Kong Carl *from Copenhagen to Kristiania in 1889.*

Opposite left: Eva Nansen (1858–1907), Fridtjof's wife.

Opposite right: Studio-posed photo of Fridtjof and Eva Nansen on skis.

At only twenty-seven years old, the handsome and self-assured blond Viking had beaten American explorer Robert Peary's attempt to cross Greenland, and he had given Norway a national champion. Nansen fever swept through Europe. The Royal Geographical Society in London awarded him the prestigious Patron's Medal in 1891.

While in Greenland, Nansen and Sverdrup had hatched a plan for their next Arctic adventure: an attempt to reach the North Pole. To trek to the very top of the world would be the biggest prize of all.

EVA

*T*HAT SAME YEAR, Nansen married Eva Sars, a celebrated concert singer. A fiercely independent thinker, Eva was the daughter of a professor of zoology and the younger sister of well-known historian Ernst Sars and marine zoologist Georg Ossian Sars. She and Nansen had met a few years before at a ski resort.

Nansen called his bride the best woman skier in Norway. At a time when women did not enter ski competitions, Eva would show up at ski-jumping events with a friend, and they were the only two women to enter the contest. Eva loved to ski into the mountains alone. When she and Nansen skied in the mountains together, the Kristiania newspapers eagerly reported on their travels.

NANSEN SETS HIS SIGHTS ON THE NORTH POLE

A **YEAR AFTER** returning from Greenland, Nansen proposed an expedition to the North Pole, but his primary goal was not merely to reach the top of the world. Even if he were to miss it by miles, he said, the success of his journey would be measured by the new scientific data he planned to collect in that little-known region.

Nansen would follow in the footsteps of his Viking ancestors, who were among the first non-native travelers to the Arctic. A Norse text from the Middle Ages contains a remarkable description of what the Vikings found:

> As soon as one has traversed the greater part of the wild sea, one comes upon such a huge quantity of ice that nowhere in the whole world has the like been known. Some of the ice ... from 8 to 10 feet thick. ... is of a wonderful nature. It lies at times quite still, as one would expect, with openings or large fjords in it; but sometimes its movement is so strong and rapid as to equal that of a ship running before the wind.

Mercator's map of the open polar sea, circa 1600.

For centuries, the world believed Arctic ice blocked a body of open water at the pole and perhaps a landmass "pushing" the ice southward. The North Pole, some speculated, might be reached through a passage of warmer north-running currents penetrating the ice. Expedition after expedition from Europe set out to find this open passageway.

In 1607, Henry Hudson attempted to reach the pole by sailing along the east coast of Greenland, but his route was blocked by ice. Hudson made another attempt along the west coast of Spitsbergen, but he came up against more ice. At the point where he turned back, Hudson had reached 79°23′ north latitude, or 637 nautical miles from the North Pole.

Fellow Englishman William Parry got stuck in the ice off the coast of the archipelago of Svalbard in 1827. Parry put boats on sleds and dragged them northward. But the south-flowing current carried the ice backward, forcing him to abandon his attempt. He made it to within 435 miles of the pole (82°45′ N), the farthest north any human had traveled to that day. Parry's achievement stood for nearly five decades, until 1876, when another British explorer, Albert Markham, despite suffering from scurvy and lack of proper clothing, traveled with dogs and sleds, and missed the pole by four hundred miles (83°20′ N).

One more northerly record was set before Nansen's quest. James Booth Lockwood on the Greely Expedition reached Mary Murray Island off northern Greenland, 396 miles from the pole (83°24′ N), just a tad closer than Markham.

Still people clung to the idea that beyond all that intractable ice, a water route could lead to the pole and beyond, perhaps even becoming a northeast passage to India. As they pushed northward, the biggest problem Arctic explorers faced was the fragility of their ships. Advancing with wooden ships a mile or two in the polar ice pack was grueling work. Most ships became frozen into the ice and were either crushed or, if lucky, dislodged after months of waiting for the ice to melt in the short Arctic summer.

The PLAN: FOLLOW the JEANNETTE

*T*O REACH THE North Pole, Nansen studied the forces of nature. Rather than going against the currents, as most other failed expeditions had done, he wanted to try something different. He would build a special ship, one strong enough to withstand the ice. He would deliberately freeze it into the northward-drifting ice pack and travel at the same slow speed that the polar current carried the ice. But he had to find the right current first—one that might take him to the top of the world—and then build a strong ship.

After much thought and investigation, Nansen was led to what he called the "Jeannette current," an east–west flow of water running across the Polar Basin. The voyage of the USS *Jeannette* (1879–81) was one of the most famous expeditions that failed to reach the North Pole. Nansen learned a lot from the ship's tragic history. Captain George De Long of the United States Navy tried a Bering Sea route to the pole because whaling ships had reported a warm northerly "Japanese" current, and De Long hoped the ice would be less severe in that direction, perhaps all the way to the pole.

It turned out to be wishful thinking. On September 6, 1879, the *Jeannette* got lodged ("nipped") into the ice near Wrangel Island, above eastern Siberia, and drifted, a frozen prisoner, for two years. De Long kept measurements of ice and weather. During his long drift, he thought it might be possible to reach the pole on the ice if they took sleds and dogs and dashed for it. But the ice eventually crushed the ship north of the New Siberian Islands, and when it sank, the thirty-three survivors, with forty dogs, dragged three small open boats southward toward the native villages of coastal Siberia a thousand miles away. While wandering through the Arctic looking for open water, they hunted polar bear and walrus to survive. (They did not eat their dogs as so many polar explorers have done to survive.) When the ice turned to water, they jumped into their leaky boats and got separated in a storm. De Long and nineteen others died. Only thirteen of the *Jeannette* crew were rescued.

That might have been the sad end of the story of the *Jeannette*—just another Arctic disaster where the ice wins out—except that three years after the *Jeannette* was destroyed, some of the sunken vessel's remains were discovered by Inuit hunters on the coast of Greenland. Apparently, the debris had been carried 2,900 miles on ice floes driven by the current across the polar basin, perhaps even coming close to the North Pole.

In 1894 Nansen read an article in a Norwegian journal by the well-known meteorologist Henrik Mohn, claiming that these "sundry articles" from the *Jeannette*, including a pair of oilskin trousers and the peak of a cap on which was written the name of a rescued crew member, must have made it to Greenland in no other way than by crossing near the North Pole on that very current. Nansen calculated the items must have traveled very slowly in the ice, perhaps only one to two miles in a twenty-four-hour period.

Nansen studied this current and was confident it existed. He found other instances of water flowing over the polar region. Among the driftwood on the coast of Greenland was found a device that Iñupiaq Eskimos used in Alaska for hunting birds; it too must have traveled on the same current as the items from the *Jeannette*.

Nansen's plan then was to drift in the same direction as the fragments of the *Jeannette* had done, from the New Siberian Islands across the pole to somewhere between Greenland and Spitsbergen (see map).

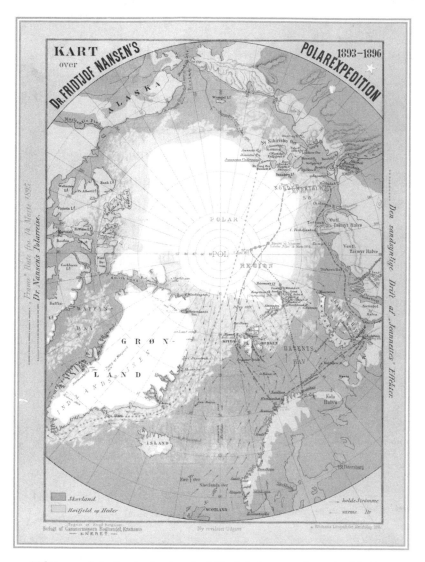

1896 map of the Arctic showing the drift of the Jeannette, *the path of the* Fram, *and Nansen's and Johansen's 15-month journey of survival.*

When he proposed the journey, almost every polar expert thought he would endanger himself and his crew in such an undertaking. Some thought he was crazy, as they had said of his previous expeditions. They thought his ship would certainly be crushed by the ice pack—if not at first, then undoubtedly later in the winter months, "when the ice resembled a mountain frozen fast to the ship's side."

In spite of near-unanimous skepticism, Nansen remained confident and proceeded with his plans.

BUILDING AN ICE SHIP

WHY DID SO many call Nansen crazy for his idea of floating—locked in ice—to the pole? After all, he'd chosen a well-respected boat builder to build the proper ship. Colin Archer was more than a shipwright; he was one of the most celebrated boat designers of his era. Archer's boats were quintessentially Norwegian and seaworthy, with the elegant, deceptively simple lines that only a people with several thousand years of living on a dangerous coast and deep fjords could create. The son of Scottish immigrants, Colin Archer was beloved in Norway. By the time he designed the *Fram*, his boats were legendary for safety.

The Fram *launching from Colin Archer's shipyard.*

One hundred twenty-eight feet long and over four hundred gross tons weight, the *Fram* (meaning "forward" in Norwegian) was a three-masted, square topsail schooner. Its massive construction was intended to serve a single purpose: to survive the enormous forces of the Arctic through all seasons, especially winter, when the deepening, ever-shifting sea ice could exert tremendous pressure on anything floating within it. Yet veteran Arctic travelers, whose ships had been nipped by the ice and whose escape to safety became heroic tales, criticized the *Fram*'s design. They had seen firsthand how their own ships crumpled like crackers in the iron fist of the ice. They had no confidence in the *Fram*, or in Nansen's plan to freeze the ship into the pack ice.

Although many tried to dissuade him, Nansen, unfazed, convinced the Norwegian government to pay for the expedition. Nansen's foresight, intelligence, planning, and leadership had gotten him across Greenland when his friends advised him against that journey. He was sure the same qualities would get him to the North Pole.

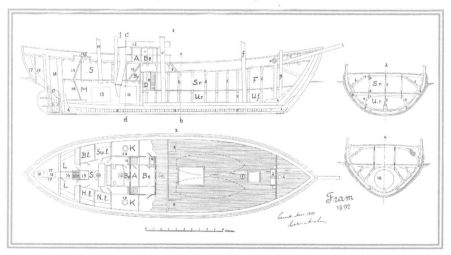

Printed replica of Archer's construction drawings of the Fram.

On the outside, the *Fram* was planked with a skin of greenheart, a dense, tropical hardwood nearly impervious to rot. Beneath, the ship consisted of multiple layers of carefully engineered wooden ingenuity—massive oak frames, oversize deck timbers, and several layers of planking. The hull shape, too, was calculated to endure. Unusually wide at thirty-four feet, it was quite round—so the pack ice would push it up instead of crushing it. The object of the ship's design, as Colin Archer explained, was to enable the whole craft "to slip like an eel out of the embraces of the ice."

The Fram, *1893.*

A CREW OF TWELVE

APPLICATIONS TO ACCOMPANY Nansen to the North Pole poured in from around the world, but Nansen chose a small, well-trained crew of twelve Norwegians for the expedition. Most of them were in their thirties. As second in command, Otto Sverdrup, now thirty-eight, would captain the ship. Nansen knew from crossing Greenland with Sverdrup that he was an experienced sailor, a proficient skier, and a good hunter. Most important, Sverdrup was calm and remarkably clearheaded under stress.

Captain Otto Sverdrup aboard the Fram.

Sigurd Scott-Hansen, as chief scientist aboard, would be in charge of keeping meteorological, astronomical, and magnetic observations. Henrik Greve Blessing—still a medical student when he applied to go on board the *Fram*—was a competent skier and would act as the ship's doctor and botanist.

Theodor Jacobsen, a flamboyant storyteller, had the most number of years at sea and would serve as chief mate under Sverdrup. Jacobsen was a talkative man with dark hair and penetrating eyes.

The oldest aboard would be the chief engineer, Anton Amundsen. At forty, Amundsen had served in the Norwegian navy for twenty-five years. Often isolated from the others, he would devote his energies to his work on the machinery aboard the *Fram*. Second engineer was Lars Pettersen, also a navy veteran, who would act as machinist and blacksmith. Hardworking and agreeable, Pettersen would be a stoker in the engine room until the *Fram* got locked into the ice and the engines were no longer needed. He would take over the cooking on the latter part of the trip.

Besides Sverdrup, Nansen had personally asked only one other person to join the *Fram*—Peder Hendriksen, who had spent twenty years at sea as a sailor, hunter, and harpooner. A good-natured man, Hendriksen loved to tell lively stories he'd collected from a rough-and-tumble career aboard sailing vessels.

As with all the men, Bernhard Nordahl, a former sailor in the navy, went aboard with multiple duties: stoker and scientific assistant, and most important as the electrician who would keep the lights shining aboard, essential for the morale of the men during the long months of winter darkness.

Ivar Mogstad was hired as carpenter and builder. He would entertain the men with his violin. He was ingenious at building things and making equipment run. He was also moody and prone to fights. Adolf Juell came aboard as cook and steward, and Bernt Bentsen signed on at the last minute. Bentsen had spent many years sailing Arctic waters.

Finally, Hjalmar Johansen had military training, was an excellent athlete, muscular, stocky, and sturdy. He had pestered Nansen to be included in the expedition until Nansen agreed to let him go in the only position available: stoker in the engine room.

Many aboard were accustomed to long sea voyages, but Nansen knew his crew would be tested by years of living in close quarters while enduring extreme cold and endless months of darkness. Nansen had wanted scientists to come along, but none applied. The men who formed his crew were a rugged bunch of characters, who Nansen prayed would find some kind of harmony during the arduous journey ahead. At the outset, he did not know how well each might perform. He wouldn't know until the *Fram* was committed to the ice, locked away for years.

The crew of the Fram *pose for a photo.*

Sitting, from left to right: *Adolf Juell, Lars Pettersen* (closest), *Bernhard Nordahl, and Peder Hendriksen.* Standing, from left to right: *Ivar Mogstad, Henrik Greve Blessing, Hjalmar Johansen, Sigurd Scott-Hansen* (sitting), *Anton Amundsen, Bernt Bentsen, Otto Sverdrup, and Theodor Jacobsen.*

Part Two

The

JOURNEY NORTH

JUNE 24, 1893—MARCH 14, 1894

The Fram *leaving Bergen and heading for the Arctic, July 2, 1893.*

LEAVING HOME

→

Kristiania, Norway
June 24, 1893

*I*N THE GLOOM of the day, Nansen said good-bye to his wife, Eva, and their six-month-old daughter, Liv. He shut the door of his house and walked alone, down through the garden to the beach, where the *Fram*'s little launch awaited him. When he caught sight of his wife and child at the window, with Liv clapping her hands, he thought, "Behind me lies all I hold dear in life."

Nansen climbed aboard the small motorboat and sped through the cold rain over Lysaker Bay. He turned his face forward into the wind.

After years of preparation, raising funds, hiring a famous boat builder to design and build a perfect ice ship, and packing enough supplies into the *Fram* for a five-year sojourn, Nansen had no real idea what was in store for him. Would this be the last time he saw his wife and daughter? Would he return home again?

Once Nansen left Norway for the frozen Arctic, all communication would end. The telephone and the telegraph had been invented, but the world had yet to see radios, cell phones, or any kind of navigation beyond celestial reckoning (see page 291). To attempt reaching the North Pole in the 1890s was like preparing for the first moon landing. Yet even Neil Armstrong, the first person to walk on the moon, was able to call his family; his moon walk was televised live in 1969. The crew of the *Fram* would be lost to the world for years.

The day the *Fram* sailed out of Kristiania harbor, Colin Archer was aboard at the helm to steer "his child." When it came time to leave the ship with the pilot, Archer shook Nansen's hand in silence. Nansen thought he might have seen a tear in Archer's old face as he stood tall in the launch heading for shore. The crew fired the ship's signal cannon for the first time, in a salute to the *Fram*'s creator.

The ship sailed up the coast. Having read in newspapers about Dr. Nansen's crazy idea of freezing his ship in the ice pack to reach the pole, people turned out in every port to celebrate Nansen and his crew. Crowds cheered; flags flew in their honor. The navy greeted them with gunboat salutes. Like other members of the expedition, Nansen enjoyed the attention, even if their premature fame seemed a little embarrassing since they had not accomplished anything yet.

Continuing up the coast, they came upon the crew of one ship who for some reason did not know who they were. From the deck came shouts of "What's your cargo? Where you bound?" Nansen's men called back, "Provisions and coal. The polar ice, the North Pole!"

The expedition took a month to travel the 1,600 miles north and then east along the coast of Norway.

In the little fishing village of Vardø, their last Norwegian port, the crew stayed up all hours and partied hard, then slept late the next morning. From the look on Nansen's face, they knew their leader did not approve. Nansen was not an easy man to get along with. Besides being separated from the others partly by education and privilege, Nansen was a man apart. Aloof as a child when he played with companions his own age, he never really made close friends the way some kids do. On board the *Fram*, Nansen, formal and serious by nature, sometimes remained separate from his crew even though he would join them in the saloon at the end of the day. They all lived physically close to one another in a series of tiny sleeping cabins crowded around the saloon table and the pot-bellied stove.

The crew eating supper on the Fram.

At three in the morning, the *Fram* weighed anchor and sailed out of Vardø harbor in silence. Johansen, the army lieutenant reservist who had joined the expedition to work in the engine room, climbed up into the crow's nest to have a last look at Norway. On deck below, Nansen gazed at the peaceful, sleeping town and felt it was just the right way to leave his beloved country, no crowds and shouts of good luck and farewell.

> *The masts in the harbor, the house-roofs, and chimneys stood out against the cool morning sky. Just then the sun broke through the mist and smiled over the shore—rugged, bare, and weather-worn in the hazy morning, but still lovely—dotted here and there with tiny houses and boats, and all Norway lay behind it. . . .*

Vardø is still a sleepy little fishing village on the edge of the Arctic Ocean and stepping-off place to Siberia.

The *Fram* slowly worked its way out to sea as Nansen watched the land fade away. He wondered what would happen to them all before they might again see "Norway rising up over the sea."

Indeed it was a cold summer that year, and the *Fram*, pushing through a never-ending fog, quickly found ice jamming the route ahead. But what an ice boat Colin Archer had made! Nansen could not have been happier. "It was a royal pleasure to work her ahead through difficult ice. She twisted and turned 'like a ball on a platter.'"

Nansen's watercolor sketch of
Off the Edge of the Ice—Gathering Storm, 14th September, 1893.

The helmsman had to labor to steer one way and then the other. When there was no avoiding it, he drove her sloping bow right up onto the ice and, with a heavy plunge, burst "the floes asunder." Even when she headed "full speed at a floe, not a creak, not a sound, is to be heard in her; if she gives a little shake it is all she does."

*Reproduction of Nansen's watercolor painting that depicts
the evening atmosphere off the Siberian coast.*

For the next two months, the *Fram* moved east and north along the coast of Siberia. Nansen took thirty-four Siberian sled dogs on board before he pointed the *Fram* northward into the ice.

THE *FRAM* LOCKED IN ICE

September 28

THERE WAS NOTHING in the world like the haunting sound of the *Fram* as it began to freeze into the pack ice. The first time she "floated" in the ice near the New Siberian Islands, Nansen heard the sound of the ship's timbers, creaking like an old barn door with rusty hinges closing slowly on a frosty night. The pack ice was trying its best to crush the ship.

Surface ice sometimes needed to be cut away and removed.

As he lay in his bunk in the dark, Nansen could hear the ice shifting a few feet from his head. He felt in his bones the monstrous power of that floating mass, tens of thousands of pounds per square foot of ice pressing against the hull. The freezing went on for weeks. Just when the crew thought the ship was frozen solid in the ice, the water would open up and the ship would slip down. Another day or two and the freezing would start again, along with the spooky sounds. After a while, the men grew accustomed to the eerie noise. They were comfortable and warm in the saloon and in their cabins because Archer had built the ceilings, floors, and walls with many thick coats of nonconducting material. The sides of the ship had been lined with tarred felt and cork padding and other layers of felt and linoleum and reindeer-hair insulation. Along with the four-inch deck planks, the total fifteen-inch thickness of the ship's walls kept the living space toasty even as the ice tried to claw its way in.

The crew relaxing in the mess on the Fram.

Nansen recorded in his journal:

The ice is restless, and has pressed a good deal to-day again. It begins with a gentle crack and moan along the side of the ship, which gradually sounds louder in every key. Now it is a high plaintive tone, now it is a grumble, now it is a snarl, and the ship gives a start up. The noise steadily grows till it is like all the pipes of an organ; the ship trembles and shakes, and rises by fits and starts, or is sometimes gently lifted. There is a pleasant, comfortable feeling in sitting listening to all this uproar and knowing the strength of our ship. Many a one would have been crushed long ago. But outside the ice is ground against our ship's sides, the piles of broken-up floe are forced under her heavy, invulnerable hull, and we lie as if in a bed. Soon the noise begins to die down; the ship sinks into its old position again, and presently all is silent as before. In several places round us the ice is piled up, at one spot to a considerable height. Towards evening there was a slackening, and we lay again in a large, open pool.

One of Nansen's journals in the archives of the National Library of Norway.

Nansen determined the ship was locked firm enough into the ice that he could move the dogs to safety off the ship's deck. The dogs had been nearly hanged from their leashes when the boat rolled violently in rough seas. When the ship stood still in ice, they barked wildly and played like mad puppies, their dark forms bouncing and springing on a sheet of white. In a few days, the crew built a dog camp on the port side and tied up all the dogs. "Our floe, a short time ago so lonesome and forlorn, was quite a cheerful sight with this sudden population; the silence of ages was broken."

The dogs' first encounter with the ice.

Nansen was always listening for any change in the pattern of sound that might indicate danger—a sudden crack or rush of water, a louder crunch than usual. Especially during that first winter, Nansen could feel the ship listing slightly to starboard as he dozed in his bunk, a listing of maybe five degrees or more until it stopped at about eight degrees. He could feel the bunk beneath his body tilting. Then, as slowly as it had listed, the ship would right itself to the sound of new, scarcely audible crunches and scrapes.

The *Fram* was fighting back.

The Fram *locked in ice.*

LIFE ABOARD THE *FRAM:* THE ADVENTURE AND MONOTONY OF BEING STUCK IN ICE

December 1893

$\mathcal{P}$OLAR BEARS PESTERED the dogs and the men. They even came on board and stole a couple of dogs at night. One cold winter evening, while the men were deep into card games in the saloon, the dogs on deck suddenly barked wildly at the darkness and jumped up on the ship's rail in their excitement. Nansen knew a polar bear was roaming around out there somewhere.

Crew reading in the engineer's quarters.

Nansen with his photography equipment.

While reading, he had heard violent scratching, a sound like boxes being dragged on deck. He discovered three dogs were missing. The other dogs went crazy, barking all night until they were set free on the ice.

Hendriksen set off in the darkness to look for the missing dogs, but soon after, he tumbled into the saloon "breathlessly shouting, 'A gun! a gun!'" A bear near the ship had bitten him in the side, not a life-threatening wound.

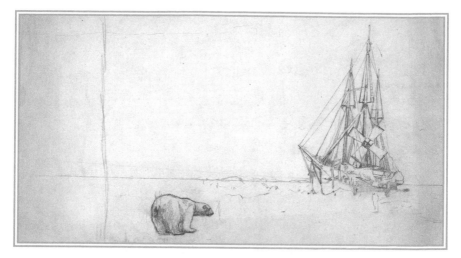

Nansen's pencil-drawn study for a lithograph of a polar bear near the Fram; *based on a photo by Nansen from March 1894.*

Nansen and Hendriksen seized their guns. They heard confused shouting and dogs barking. Hendriksen shouted, "Shoot. Shoot." His gun had jammed. The men saw a bear chewing on one of the dogs a little way off on the ice. Nansen's gun also didn't work. Other guns weren't working. Now there were four men "and not one that could shoot, although we could have prodded the bear's back with our gun-barrels."

Scott-Hansen's observatory for magnetic measuring, made of ice blocks next to the Fram.

Scott-Hansen groped in the chart room for cartridges, and at last, Johansen appeared and "sent a ball straight down into the bear's hide."

All that did, however, was make the bear growl as he let go of the dog. A few more shots, and the bear lay still on the ice. The dogs stood quietly in front of the dead animal. It was only a thin little bear that had caused all the commotion.

Nansen now set off in the darkness to look for the three missing dogs. He could barely make out the shadows of the dogs he took with him when they quickly caught a scent, grew frightened, and refused to go any farther. Nansen crawled over the rough pack ice with his gun at the ready, expecting any moment for a bear to charge him. He sensed he was coming up to something, then found one of the missing dogs, mangled and frozen stiff; then another dog in a pool of blood whose head had been partly eaten.

H. Egidius's drawing of Suddenly she halted, let the cubs go on in front, sniffed a little, *based on a photo by Nansen.*

Johansen held his lantern over the third dog. "Flesh and skin and entrails were gone; there was nothing to be seen but a bare breast and back-bone, with some stumps of ribs. It was a pity that the fine strong dog should come to such an end. . . ."

In fact, this particular dog was one of the few "bad-tempered" dogs that always growled and barked at Johansen, who was a good dog handler. Nansen wondered if Johansen was glad the dog was dead now. "No, I am sorry," said the kindhearted Johansen, "because we did not make it up before he died."

Dogs by the ship.

Nansen smokes a pipe near the Fram.
Dog and bearskins hang to dry alongside the ship.

January 1894

Nansen often dreamed of home. Day after day, with the same monotonous routine aboard, locked into that ice desert, Nansen thought, *Why does home seem so far away? . . . life without it is so empty, so empty.* He especially longed for home when the *Fram* started drifting backward instead of north. The ship drifted with its bow facing south for days on end, and Nansen's heart grew heavy. His dream of reaching the pole, battling so much ice, seemed futile. But then the ship would suddenly start to drift northward again, and with the change came a renewed hope.

Nansen in his cabin.

The crew around the supper table, on board the Fram.
From the left in front: *Lars Pettersen and Anton Amundsen.*
In the back from the left: *Bernhard Nordahl, Ivar Otto Irgens Mogstad,
Peder Leonard Hendriksen, Adolf Juell, and Bernt Bentsen.*

Nansen described the endless loneliness aboard his ship, which was like a fossil in all that ice:

> *I gaze into the far distance, far over the barren plain of snow, a boundless, silent, and lifeless mass of ice in imperceptible motion. No sound can be heard save the faint murmur of the air through the rigging, or perhaps far away the low rumble of packing ice. In the midst of this empty waste of white there is but one little dark spot, and that is the* Fram.

The Fram *locked in ice, with Nansen's giant windmill on deck.*

Imprisoned during the polar darkness of winter, the ship was nevertheless lit up inside like a Christmas tree with electric lights powered by an enormous windmill that Nansen had erected on deck. Electric lights. The expedition leader had thought of everything. And as long as the windmill worked, the artificial lights helped the men through the loneliness.

Hjalmar Johansen and Sigurd Scott-Hansen playing halma, a strategy board game.

At night there were happy sounds from the crew joking and telling stories in the warm, dry, and bright saloon while the ever-shifting ice piled up around them like castle walls. The food was so good that Nansen had to institute regular bouts of exercise so the men would stay in shape.

Crew skiing to the Fram.

A typical lunch, the big meal of the day that they called *middag*, or "dinner," consisted of three courses: soup, meat, and dessert; or soup, fish, and meat with potatoes, and either green vegetables or macaroni. Nansen thought the food might be better aboard the *Fram* than some of the crew ate at home.

Crew member Adolf Juell cooked and baked. Part farmer, part seaman, he had learned to cook from his wife, and he was particularly passionate about baking fresh rolls for breakfast.

Doghouse on the ice.

After lunch, the men took a nap and then went back to chores. Hundreds of daily tasks aboard included feeding and exercising the dogs, working in the galley, washing dishes, repairing the engine, making axe handles, inspecting the hull and engines, soldering loose joints, making canvas boots, and fixing scientific instruments. (See Duties of the Crew Aboard, page 263.)

Cleaning batteries near the forge.

The men worked until six o'clock, when they sat down to another meal, which they called "supper." The menu consisted of both rye and wheat bread, various cheeses, corned beef or corned mutton, ham, bacon, cod caviar, anchovy roe, oatmeal biscuits, and jelly. Nansen also brought half a ton of cloudberry jam (a fruit like a raspberry or blackberry) and a great variety of canned vegetables.

Henrik Greve Blessing, Sigurd Scott-Hansen, and Otto Sverdrup playing cards in the ship's lounge.

The crew enjoyed reading from an extensive library of over four hundred books. The men played games and cards in groups around the saloon table until well into the night. Nansen might crank up the organ, or Johansen would pull out his accordion to perform "Oh! Susanna" over and over again. Mogstad played the violin.

Fridtjof Nansen playing the organ.

Yet no amount of music and electric light over so many months could soften the "cold prison of loneliness" of being wedged in ice. Tensions between the men flared up occasionally but mostly simmered beneath the surface.

Nansen recorded the restlessness everyone felt:

We are lying motionless—no drift. . . . this inactive, lifeless monotony, without any change, wrings one's very soul. No struggle, no possibility of struggle! . . . the very soul freezes. What would I not give for a single day of struggle—for even a moment of danger!

Nansen craved action, and soon he would have more danger than he could desire.

Men resting on the deck of the Fram, Arctic Ocean, June 16, 1894.

Reproduction of Nansen's pastel: Ice near the *Fram*, 4th July, 1894.

Nansen inspecting the temperature from the water dipper.

SCIENCE ABOARD

May 10

*E*VEN AS HE chafed at the chains of monotony on board the *Fram*, Nansen never neglected his science. He retrieved samples of water in special metal tubes he was inventing to capture water at specific depths (later called Nansen bottles). He dropped nets

Water sampler that Anton Amundsen helped build aboard the Fram.

through the ice to collect marine animals and shells; he measured the depth of the floor of the Arctic Ocean, sometimes running out of line trying to reach almost two and a half miles down.

Sounding the depth of the Polar Sea to 3500 meters (over 2 miles deep).

Nansen wrote in his diary, "I do not think we shall talk any more about the shallow Polar Sea, where land may be expected anywhere. We may very possibly drift out into the Atlantic Ocean without having seen a single mountain-top." So much for the age-old notion that there was some sort of landmass at the North Pole as there is at the South Pole, where a thick layer of ice covers a continental landmass. By testing the depths of the water below the ice, Nansen was discovering irrefutable evidence that the region of the North Pole was only a cap of ice sitting atop a deep polar sea.

Johansen (left) *assisting Scott-Hansen with scientific observations.*

Meteorological readings, some of the most exacting scientific observations made aboard the *Fram*, needed to be done every four hours. Johansen would first read the thermometer and other instruments on deck, then those in the saloon. These were followed by readings in the crow's nest to get an air sample from a higher stratum. Johansen then went onto the ice to read more instruments. Every second day, as a rule, he would help with astronomical observations to decide the ship's location in its slow progress across the Polar Sea.

Nansen found himself often lost in study outside the usual framework of time. "Here I sit," he said, ". . . and shut myself up in the snail-shell of my studies. Day after day I dive down into the world of the microscope, forgetful of time and surroundings."

Nansen and crew resting on the Fram's *afterdeck.*

After a while, the men took their safety for granted, although Nansen knew the ice could crush them at any moment. Nansen wrote:

> *Should the ship be crushed in this ice and go to the bottom, like the Jeannette, without our being able to save sufficient supplies to continue our drift on the ice, we should have to turn our course to the south, and then there would be little doubt as to our fate. The Jeannette people fared badly enough, but their ship went down in 77° north latitude, while the nearest land to us is many times more than double the distance it was in their case, to say nothing of the nearest inhabited land.*

The speed and direction of the *Fram*'s drifting, although heading mostly north and northwest, was anything but uniform. Sometimes the ship drifted forward; other times, back again. On a map, the journey looked like "a confusion of loops and knots." A man with any less of a sense of discipline might easily have gone mad from restlessness.

Nansen observes the solar eclipse with Johansen and Scott-Hansen.
From left to right: Hjalmar Johansen, Fridtjof Nansen, and Sigurd Scott-Hansen.

Johansen and Scott-Hansen examining the barometers on board.

Crew on skis with dogs.

DECISION TO LEAVE THE SHIP

December 31, New Year's Eve, 1894

NANSEN MADE A toast in the saloon. He said that 1894 had gone well because everyone got along even in such a small ship. Yes, he said, of course there had been some tensions and frictions; each crew member had gone through his own dark hours, but this, he said, was bound to happen. Everyone had a good understanding of one another, he thought.

January 5, 1895

The *Fram* was now locked in ice twenty to thirty feet thick, exposed to the greatest pressures of the entire trip. The ice piled up above the deck high into the rigging, "threatening, if not to crush her, at least to bury her." Everyone on board was worried the *Fram* might finally get crushed, and so preparations were made to abandon ship.

Baro (left) *and Suggen greet Adolf Juell.*

Nansen required the crew to sleep fully clothed in case they had to run for it. They piled provisions and cooking utensils and sleds and kayaks out on the ice. And they listened to such creaks and groans as would fill a soul with horror, but Colin Archer's boat withstood the monstrous compressions of the winter pack ice. (Later,

Nansen and his crew were unable to find a single crack or splinter in her splendid hull as she continued on her northward drift.)

Outdoor life around the Fram.

For some time, Nansen had known the *Fram* would miss the actual point on the globe that is the pole, maybe by as much as three hundred miles. He had been thinking about leaving the ship to make a dash for it, sure he could get there with dogs and sleds if he traveled light and with only one companion. It meant the two of them would have to leave the ship for good. Yes, he had always said the primary purpose of the expedition was to study the science of the unknown Arctic, and they were indeed collecting massive amounts of new information on temperatures, water composition, ocean depths, currents, and ice conditions. But to be the first to reach the North Pole was a tempting challenge, and now was his only chance.

In the darkness of their second winter, Nansen and Sverdrup skied under moonlight. They talked about Nansen making a run for the pole. Sverdrup supported the idea. All the scientific observations would continue aboard the *Fram*, as usual, Sverdrup said, whether Nansen was there or not.

The Fram *packed in ice at night.*

Nansen had to choose the right companion for the trip. He knew from their Greenland experience that Otto Sverdrup would be perfect, but Nansen also knew that he had to leave the *Fram* in Sverdrup's capable command. Other crew members showed interest. A few might have made excellent companions. Peder Hendriksen, for example, had been a harpooner on whaling ships and was a good shipmate, who desperately wanted to go along, but in the end Nansen chose Hjalmar Johansen, "a fine fellow, physically and mentally." Johansen was steadfast, a champion athlete, and an extremely competent skier.

Officer Hjalmar Johansen, meteorological assistant and stoker.

Nansen was impressed by the twenty-six-year-old's quiet, unassuming good nature. Johansen had worked hard through two polar winters: first in the hot engine room as the seas rolled and he got seasick for weeks, and then at every task he undertook.

Johansen, for his part, was a little wary of traveling with the expedition leader. Many aboard called Nansen "Himself," and they grumbled that Nansen always had an opinion about things and wanted to be right about everything. Nansen stood apart from the men in a way that the more compatible Sverdrup did not. In fact, some even looked forward to Nansen leaving the ship.

Lars Pettersen in the Arctic.

Johansen was from a very different background than Nansen. He was the son of a caretaker, who had wanted Hjalmar to enter the military academy. Johansen studied law instead, but did not perform well and dropped out of law school to work after his father died. In addition to being a strong skier, Johansen had represented Norway in gymnastics at the 1889 world's fair in Paris.

Johansen with Sultan the dog by the Fram.

Nansen knew that he and Johansen could die on the upcoming dash to the pole, so he wrote a letter to his wife, Eva, to prepare her for the worst:

> *You will know that your image will be the last I see . . . when I go to the eternal rest, where we will meet some time and rest for ever safely in each other's arms. Ah Eva, my Eva, if it should happen, do not cry too hard. Remember no one escapes his fate.*

Eva and Fridtjof Nansen.

Nansen was plagued by worry as he planned for the journey. His emotions seemed like a roller coaster of excitement and doubt. He would stroll on deck every morning with "an exulting feeling of triumph, deep in the soul, a feeling that all one's dreams are about to be realized with the rising sun," then he would be overwhelmed by sadness and a sense of loss at the thought of leaving his ship-mates. His eyes would wander over the map of the Arctic on the wall in his cabin, and he would get a chill at the thought of wandering out into the solitude of the frozen wasteland.

Since they could never again find the *Fram* in that vast desert of ice once they had reached their goal, Nansen and Johansen would need to turn south and locate Franz Josef Land, a set of 191 tiny, mostly unmapped islands in an archipelago about 560 miles from the pole. The cartographer Julius Payer first began to chart these islands on board the *Admiral Tegetthoff* in 1873, only twenty years before. Payer had called the area the kingdom of the dead, but Nansen knew there would be plenty of polar bears, walrus, and seals to hunt.

The area had been visited only a few times. The maps were not accurate, and there were several islands marked that did not exist, islands farther north and west of Franz Josef Land that Nansen thought would act more like stepping-stones for his journey back to Svalbard.

Even so, Nansen studied every documented detail. His and Johansen's survival would depend on Nansen's knowledge.

Otto Sverdrup notes Scott-Hansen's observations.

Part Three

OUTFITTING

for a

TWO-MAN DASH

FEBRUARY 1895

PREPARATIONS

→

NANSEN AND THE crew worked day and night in preparation for Nansen and Johansen's dash to the pole. Nansen's head was filled "with everything that must be done and not forgotten." He became more on edge as time got closer to departure, and his overbearing nature sometimes irritated the men. Johansen kept wondering if traveling alone with the leader would go well.

Preparations continued, along with a plan. The three sleds would be loaded with 1,500 pounds of gear and supplies in canvas bags. The food would keep the two men alive for one hundred days. Nansen hoped to reach the pole (360 nautical miles away) in thirty days, but would allow for fifty for the trip north, and fifty additional days heading south to look for land. Nansen also knew he could not pack enough food to feed all twenty-eight dogs for the same one hundred days. The loads on the sleds would become too heavy. So he planned to haul only a thirty-day supply of dog food, and when the food ran out for the dogs, he would have to feed any sick or weak dog to the others. He and Johansen had to keep the healthy dogs pulling the sleds, or the journey would fail. To save ammunition for polar bears and walrus, they would use a knife to take the life of a dog that could not pull anymore. Neither man relished this gruesome idea, but Nansen, who had made precise calculations, knew how much each dog weighed and how long the others could travel on their companions' flesh. And if their supplies ran out, the two men could boil up some dog-blood porridge, a mixture of blood, powdered fish, cornmeal, and blubber, to eat as they traveled on the ice.

Baro the dog.

This was a reality of Arctic travel back then, and there was no protection for animals as there is today. Sled dogs were the only means of traveling long distances on the ice. Dogs made polar exploration possible in the nineteenth and early twentieth centuries. Today's explorers to the pole do not treat dogs as polar explorers did in the past, nor do they either eat their dogs or feed dogs to other dogs. (On his 1986 sled journey to the North Pole, explorer Geoff

Carroll kept his teams of huskies alive and well. You can read more about what a modern polar journey with sled dogs is like on page 285.)

Careful planning had to go into what to eat on the sled trip. Variety was crucial. In case they lost their stove or ran out of fuel, the food had to be edible without needing to be cooked. To keep overall weight to a minimum, the food was dried. To get the meat in the right condition for travel, ox muscle with no fat or gristle was dried quickly to keep it fresh, then ground down into powder and mixed with beef suet. Nansen would take thirty-four pounds of fish flour, which they planned to boil in water and mix with corn or wheat flour and butter or dried potatoes for "an appetizing dish." The flour had been pre-steamed and could be eaten without preparation of any kind. Dried boiled potatoes, pea soup, chocolate, and a thick salty meat extract added variety to their diet. For bread, they carried dried wheat biscuits, combined with eighty-six pounds of concentrated butter.

The crew preparing the lifeboat for sailing.

TENT

NANSEN DESIGNED A special tent for this trip. Made of silk, it weighed only three pounds. Square at the bottom and pointed at the top, it was supported by a single pole in the middle and secured in the ice with sixteen tent pegs. It had no floor, so it would not collect snow from their boots as they walked in and out; such unwanted snow would have melted at night, adding even more weight to the sleds.

CLOTHING

LAYERS. NANSEN INTRODUCED the idea of wearing layers of clothes for polar travel. The two men could add layers if they were cold, or take them off, one or two layers at a time, if they overheated with vigorous exercise in rising outside temperatures. In a typical day, Nansen planned to wear a camel-hair jacket over two wool shirts, with a thick wool sweater on the outside. He and Johansen also had layers for their legs: long woolen underwear, then knickerbockers (baggy trousers gathered at the knee or calf) and loose Norwegian homespun gaiters (worn to cover the ankles and lower legs). For protection from the wind and fine driven snow, they wore a thin cotton canvas suit of wide overalls. In addition to snow goggles, their felt hats would shade their eyes from the piercing Arctic sunlight. Over the hats they draped one or two cloth hoods to regulate the warmth of their heads.

Footgear would also be crucial for the trek to the pole. Nansen knew the best boot for traveling over ice and snow was something called the Finn shoe, made from the skin of the hind legs of a reindeer buck. The Finn shoe required a lot of care at the end of the day. In warmer weather, they could turn the shoes inside out to dry on a ski pole in the sun and wind. In colder temperatures, they would need to brush off the snow before taking the shoes inside their sleeping bag to dry during the night. In the coldest temperatures, they would sleep with the shoes on their feet.

They planned to follow the Sami practice of filling their shoes with "sennegrass," a particular kind of Arctic grass that could wick away the moisture from their skin. When the grass got wet and began to clump after weeks of use, it would have to be pulled out at night and dried separately inside a coat or trouser leg and then pressed back into the boot in the morning. When the grass lost all its properties over time, they would replace it with fresh grass Nansen had brought along. For warmer temperatures, he had *komagers*, a type of moccasin the Sami people wear in summer, rubbed with tar and tallow to make them pliable and durable. The soles were fashioned from the skin of the blue seal.

Their socks, warm and durable, made of sheep's wool and human hair, like almost everything else, had to go into their sleeping bag at night to dry (as did their large wolf-skin gloves and woolen mittens).

Dog-drawn sleds returning to the Fram.

DOUBLE SLEEPING BAG

*P*ERHAPS THE SINGLE most important item for the trip would be their double sleeping bag, which was also Nansen's invention, like the three-man bags he used on his Greenland trip. One notable feature was the closeable hood that retained the heat inside. In the months leading up to the trek, Nansen had instructed Sverdrup to join two single-man sleeping bags and reverse the reindeer fur to the inside, and then enlarge the bag so it could fit two men fully dressed. The importance of the heat that would be generated inside their bag could not be emphasized enough. Although nothing ever thoroughly dried, the bag would be the single method for more or less drying everything from boots and socks to pants and coats and hats, before the men would get up again and hit the freezing trail.

Dog on the ice, with the meteorological station in the distance.

SLEDS, KAYAKS, AND GUNS

➤

NANSEN PATTERNED THE three sleds, or sledges as he called them, on those he devised for his Greenland trek. The broad fat runners moved smoothly over rough ice. He chose leather, instead of metal, to lash all the parts of the sled together and make them more flexible, less liable to break under harsh conditions. The sleds (two weighed seventy-seven pounds; the third came in at forty-four pounds) were long and narrow and could turn with ease over the many irregularities of ridges, bumps, and cracks.

Dogsledding, September 28, 1894.

Traveling across the ice.

Nansen took the dogs for trial runs that maddened him when the sled turned over, the equipment fell out, and he got dragged by the dogs. Sometimes the dogs broke into horrible fights, one fastening his teeth onto another's hide. It was hard to separate the fighting dogs, but gradually Nansen's skills as a dog musher improved.

Drawing by A. Bloch of
My first attempt at dog driving.

Attached to the underside of the sleds were spare sets of skis. Nansen knew the skis would get worn down in the wet, granular snow of the upcoming summer, so they were made from durable hardwoods like hickory. Mogstad worked on an odometer device

Nansen called a sledgemeter, made from a wheel mounted on the back of one of the sleds to measure the distance traveled.

Nansen secured two sixteen-pound, canvas-covered, Inuit-style kayaks on top of the piles of gear so that when the polar spring arrived in a few months and the ice turned to frozen slush, he and Johansen could quickly launch these easy-to-handle boats in the open water. He had learned from the Greenland Inuit just how speedy and handy these native boats were. They could also be used for fishing and hunting.

Since the two men would travel over vast expanses of ice where polar bears, walrus, and seals roamed, along with many birds, Nansen brought two guns, each of which had two barrels, one that could shoot a big bullet and the other that could fire cartridges. The two different types of barrel, rifle and shotgun, would allow them to hunt any game they encountered. For ammunition, they brought nearly two hundred bullets (for big game) and around one hundred fifty shot cartridges (mostly for birds).

COOK KIT
AND MEDICINE

⟶

*T*HE **PRIMUS STOVE** was a newly marketed device that efficiently burned kerosene as fuel. It was reliable and durable, and worked well in adverse conditions. Nansen would use it for cooking and for melting ice into large quantities of water that the two men needed for drinking at the end of the day and in the morning before they set out.

Together with two tin mugs, tin spoons, and a tin ladle, the stove kit weighed just under nine pounds. They also brought sufficient fuel, which they hoped would last at least one hundred days for cooking two hot meals a day.

Nansen packed a medical kit, which included essential drugs, splints, plaster-of-Paris bandages for possible broken legs and arms, medication for toothaches, and a couple of curved needles and some silk for sewing up wounds. Dr. Blessing gave Nansen and Johansen a quick course in setting broken limbs. One of the real dangers of Arctic travel was frostbite, damage to skin caused by extreme cold (fingers, toes, and noses are most often affected), so Nansen brought a scalpel, two large artery tweezers, and the colorless liquid chloroform, used in those days as a general anesthetic, in case one of their limbs needed amputation.

Opposite: *This photo was taken during the polar bear hunt. A rifle appears on the bottom right.*

Observing the solar altitude.

INSTRUMENTS FOR NAVIGATION

SCOTT-HANSEN TAUGHT JOHANSEN the basics of navigation, and they took instruments to get readings from the sun
and stars that determined their position: a small theodolite weighing
just over two pounds, a pocket sextant, an artificial glass horizon, an
aluminum azimuth compass, and a few extra small compasses. (See
page 289 for more on navigating in the Arctic). For observations of
the weather, they carried various barometers, thermometers, and
other instruments. To all of this, they added a telescope, a camera,
and of course notebooks to keep their daily journals.

Part Four

ONTO *the* ICE

MARCH 14–APRIL 6, 1895

*This is the final group photograph before Nansen and Johansen
take off toward the North Pole.*

EACH MILE A NEW RECORD

→

$\mathcal{B}$EFORE NANSEN AND Johansen left the ship, the *Fram* reached the farthest north any human had ever traveled (84° north latitude, or 360 nautical miles from the pole), beating Lockwood's record for the Greely Expedition by thirty-six miles. Also, the giant red rim of the sun rose above the horizon for the first time that year.

The crew of the *Fram* fired a farewell cannon salute. The wind shredded the shouts of good-bye and good luck.

Snow, sky—a blast of hazy white ahead—the ice stretched out in all directions, seemingly forever. Nansen skied out front. The dogs yipped at the wind that whipped their ears. Johansen shouted "*Sass!*"—which meant "Mush!" in the Sami language.

When the twenty-eight dogs jerked the sled runners free, the yelping ceased. The dogs started to tug the heavy loads, slowly at first, then faster as they worked in unison.

Finally, after eighteen snail-crawling months aboard the *Fram*, Nansen was thrilled to be leaving the ship, his third and final attempt to set out. Two previous attempts had ended in returning to the ship to reduce the number of sleds, lighten the loads, and fix broken equipment. Johansen had thought it odd that Nansen should make so many changes to their gear at the very last minute. In fact, Johansen continued to wonder what it would be like to travel with Mr. Nansen, as he called the expedition leader. Nansen, always capable and industrious, could be severe and moody in his drive to succeed.

The last hour before Nansen and Johansen's departure.
(H. Johansen second from the left, *and Fridtjof Nansen* second from the right*).*

At −42° Celsius, or −43.6° Fahrenheit, the deep cold made the snow as slick as sand. The slightest incline brought the sleds to an abrupt halt. Finding reliable footing to start up again was extremely difficult. One sled kept tumbling over. The two men strained to get it righted, only to be disappointed as it toppled again.

Supporting their comrades, five of their shipmates chose to start out with Nansen and Johansen, to keep them company for a few miles. Sverdrup and Mogstad were the first to turn back. Mogstad left with one broken ski because Johansen had already broken one of his skis in the first few miles and now borrowed one from Mogstad.

The other three—Scott-Hansen, Hendriksen, and Pettersen—traveled the entire seven miles of the first day and slept beside Nansen's tent in a snow hut they built around their skis and poles.

Settling down for the night, the dogs dug nests in the snow and curled up with their tails over their noses and feet to keep them from freezing.

After breakfast the three loyal shipmates helped lash all the gear onto the sleds and harness the yelping dogs. They shook hands one last time, then turned back toward the ship.

In the distance, Peder Hendriksen stood on top of an ice hummock, watching the two men and twenty-eight dogs disappear into the frozen wasteland. Nansen wondered what Peder could be thinking. Perhaps he was sad because he might never see Nansen and Johansen again.

Peder Leonard Hendriksen gazing at the Fram.

Nansen led his team out front, his sled pulled by Kvik (Quick), Baro, Lilleræven (Little Fox), Sjøliget (Strumpet), Narrifas (Trickster), Freia, Barbara, Potiphar, and Klapperslangen (Rattlesnake). The middle sled was pulled by Suggen (Thug), Baby, Haren (Hare), Gulen (Yellow), Flint, Kaifas, Blok (Block), Bjelki, and Sultan. Johansen followed up in the rear with Barabbas, Kvindfolket (Woman), Perpetuum, Katta (Cat), Livjægeren (Life Hunter), Storræven (Big Fox), Russen (the Russian), Isbjørn (Polar Bear), Pan, and Ulenka.

When the ice flattened out, Nansen found comfort in the sound of the dogs panting and the tread of their padded feet as they pulled the sleds across smoother ice. Then, suddenly, the ice vanished. At the edge of a long arm of open water, called a *lead*, the wind and sea currents had pulled apart separate ice floes the size of city blocks.

Nansen could see the water opening up in front of him. Even at −40°C (−40°F), the Arctic pack ice was in constant motion. To continue north, they would have to detour around the widening lead, their journey zigzagging to avoid water lanes that kept appearing and disappearing.

Nansen drove his sled into the knifing wind, looking for a safe place to cross. The ice froze his eyelashes. He battled to keep his eyes open to see where he was going. When his eyes froze shut, he rubbed them with his big wolf-skin gloves.

"*Sass!*" Nansen shouted at the struggling dogs. "*Sass!*" But the dogs halted once again. Jumbled ridges of frozen ocean as high as houses blocked their route north. Here was a preview of hazards to come and the months of backbreaking work ahead. These massive ice formations, or *pressure ridges* as they are known to Arctic explorers, are the nightmare of polar travel. A pressure ridge is the big frozen hill that forms when two sheets, or pans, of ice are pressed together.

The men began to work the first sled inch by inch over the crest, keeping a line on the sled to prevent it from tumbling over. But it was useless. The weight of the supplies toppled the sled again, and fragments of ice tore into the fragile canvas kayak, ripping it badly and making it unseaworthy.

If they could just lighten their loads, Nansen thought, how much faster the sleds would move. Yet he knew it would be weeks before the dogs and the men could eat enough supplies to make the sleds lighter and easier to work over these ridges.

Nansen and Johansen lifting a sledge over rough ice.

Nansen's hands ached whenever he took off his gloves to untangle the dogs' traces (the leather straps connecting the dogs to one another and to the sled). Cracking his whip, shouting at the dogs, throwing his shoulders into his work, thirty-three-year-old Fridtjof Nansen strained to lift his heavy sled over the endless blocks of ice.

Even with his single focus on moving forward, a small part of him, he admitted, longed to be back on the *Fram*, sitting in the warm saloon by the sizzling, potbellied stove, enjoying the laughter and company of the crew. That camaraderie of his men had helped him during the long, slow drift of the *Fram* through two polar winters, when the sun refused to rise above the horizon. But this, too, felt good, to be moving again, with the sun returning to the sky.

After battling the ice for hours, the dogs and the men needed rest. When they found a place to camp behind a ridge of ice, out of the wind, Johansen tied up and fed the dogs while Nansen pitched the tent and filled the pot with ice to melt. He lit the burner and started supper, a Norwegian stew of pemmican and dried potatoes.

They huddled together in the midst of the frozen polar sea, as the wind screamed and the tent flapped so loudly that the men had to shout to be heard. Johansen stepped outside and began pacing back and forth to warm his stiffened limbs. As Nansen smoked his pipe, he knew this run to the pole might be a fool's mission. It was certainly a race against time. The short Arctic summer would be here soon, and the ice would break up. Could they reach the North Pole, then turn south to find land, in only one hundred days?

That night Nansen and Johansen wedged themselves fully dressed into the tight double sleeping bag, their bodies snug together, their frozen clothes slowly melting around them. Since the two men preferred not to sleep face-to-face in such close quarters, whenever one man turned over, the other man turned over too. They turned and turned, their breath steaming up the bag, moistening it from the inside out. With little way to dry the bag the next day, the moisture would freeze, adding weight that the dogs had to tug valiantly over the ridges.

The two men haul their kayaks over the pressure ridges.

THE COLD

March 18

*A*T −40°C (−40°F), it took a lot of effort to get up and hit the trail. Johansen tossed and turned, and turned over one more time before jumping out of the bag to start the stove. The two men ate oatmeal in silence. They spent hours lashing their gear and harnessing the dogs, whose double coats of fur, one outer to keep the snow away from their bodies and the other a waterproof inner coat for insulation, had kept them warm throughout the night in the snow nests they dug.

Nansen made sure the lashings were tight. Everything had to be tied down correctly for the rugged trek. The dogs yipped and danced about, anxious to move forward. The eagerness of the dogs cheered the men onward.

Drawing by Nansen: Traveling smoother ground.

"*Sass! Sass!*" Nansen shouted, and off they went over a bit of smooth ice. The dogs seemed to be in good spirits. They loved running in harness; they were born to pull. Their body heat and hot breath formed clouds of fog as they pumped and clawed at the ice. The two men were averaging about nine miles a day when a frozen spike tore a big hole in a sack of fish flour. All the precious food sifted onto the snow.

For an hour they gathered up as much flour as they could, shooing away the dogs, then continued onward until the sledgemeter broke against a frozen ledge. They lashed it together. Then Nansen discovered he had left his pocket compass on a hummock on the trail. Johansen volunteered to go back to retrieve it.

The next day the sledgemeter fell off somewhere along the trail, and Nansen decided it would be useless to go back and look for it. Now they would no longer know the exact distance they traveled on the ice each day.

They were delayed when the first dog grew sick and was unable to pull a sled. Livjægeren (pronounced **leave-YA-ger-en**) was nearly strangled in the traces, and Johansen had to cut him free so the other dogs would not trample him to death. After that, Livjægeren roamed loose until the men realized they had not seen him in hours. Nansen skied back to their previous campsite to fetch the sick dog, who had curled up on the spot where the tent had been pitched.

A week after leaving the *Fram*, the weather was perfect for traveling, clear skies and brilliant orange sunsets. But the sun was very low on the horizon and not very intense, so it remained cold all day. From the hard work of travel, their sweat seeped through layer upon layer of clothing, until even their outer clothes turned into suits of ice armor.

Two dogs on the ice.

Temperatures are relative traveling in the Arctic. Under normal circumstances, −40°C (−40°F) might feel miserable, but here at the top of the world, it seemed bearable. When the two men stopped to camp, the deep cold froze their noses and made them ache all over.

Some nights they made a meal of flour, butter, and fishmeal. Other nights, a soup of peas, beans, or lentils with bread and pemmican. Then they dove for what Nansen called their "dear" sleeping bag. At first, it was painful to wear those layers of stiff clothes inside the bag. But the bag was always the reward after a long, hard day's work.

The frozen sleeve of Nansen's coat rubbed deep sores into his wrist. Frostbite had nearly reached the bone. In Nansen's day, frostbite was treated by warming the affected skin slowly, rubbing it with snow or immersing it in cold water. Today, frostbite is treated differently; much more of the tissue can be saved if the affected parts are warmed quickly, as in a hot bath if it's available, which of course for Nansen it was not. Johansen's finger also got frostbitten, so Nansen rubbed it with snow to get it working again.

One clear morning, the travel seemed so easy that Nansen had the hopeful idea they could reach the pole in much less time than he'd planned.

"*Sass!*" Johansen's voice grew hoarse from shouting at the dogs. His back ached from the heavy work of maneuvering the sleds over ridges of slabs and righting the sleds when they toppled over.

FIRST DOG *to* DIE

→

March 24

*T*HE SLEDS CAME to an abrupt stop in front of a wall of ice. The dogs, as usual, had been eager that morning to begin the journey, but now they suddenly refused to pull. Yipping and yowling, they jumped over one another's traces, making a tangled mess. Even though it was −45°C (−49°F), the men took off their gloves and, with frozen, bleeding fingers, untangled the lines. This was the worst ice encountered so far.

Fighting a stiff northeast wind, they lifted the sleds over pressure ridges, making only a few miles that day. Even so, Nansen was encouraged by the lengthening hours of daylight, which meant they could travel almost any time of day or night. Soon it would be polar day, that strange occurrence near the poles when the sun never sets. That is why the Arctic is called the "Land of the Midnight Sun." From mid-April until mid-September, at the latitude where they were traveling, the sun does not set, but circles above the horizon all day long.

When Livjægeren grew too weak to pull, Nansen made the difficult decision to let him go. He was the first of the twenty-eight dogs to die. Nansen admitted this was "some of the most disagreeable work" he had to do on the whole trip, particularly at the beginning of the journey.

When they passed out the cut-up remains of Livjægeren to the other dogs to eat, some chose to go without supper. As the trip progressed, however, the weary dogs would get much hungrier.

Nansen and Johansen turned away their eyes and hardened their hearts. They loved their dogs and treated them well when they were traveling, but if one grew too weak to pull, it became food to keep the other dogs alive and to make this trip possible. Survival depended on a dog's ability to pull.

Their sleds and kayaks.

THE ICE, THE ROUTINE, THE DOGS

March 28

NANSEN GREW SO exhausted that his eyes closed, his head dropped to his chest, and he slept as he trudged along, only to be awakened when he fell forward on his skis. The cold, damp nights kept the travelers awake even when they tried to sleep in the bag.

The two men aimed for nine or ten hours of travel a day. They rarely spoke to each other as they worked their sleds over the ice fields, the teams sometimes getting separated by hundreds of yards. For short breaks, they would come together to sit on their sleds or the sleeping bag, roll themselves up in blankets, and in silence eat a lunch of bread and butter, adding a little pemmican or liver pâté. For extra energy, they might gobble a few chunks of meat-chocolate. When the temperature from the windchill dropped below −51°C (−60°F), they paced back and forth, eating as they walked.

To avoid the famous Arctic thirst that had plagued so many northern sled journeys, when men were working so hard their bodies became wet with perspiration, each man carried a flask of water inside their jackets to keep it from freezing. Unlike in Greenland, however, Nansen found he hardly needed water at all and was satisfied sucking on a piece of ice during the day.

A few dogs gnawed through their traces and got loose, and the men scrambled to catch them. This wasn't so easy. They spliced the tattered traces together. One of the dogs, Russen, was so challenging, they made his harness out of wire, but he managed to gnaw the traces of another dog and set that one free. Much time was lost when dogs got loose.

Nansen took a navigational reading to discover they were only at 85°30′N, or two hundred seventy nautical miles from the pole. He had thought for sure they'd be thirty-five miles farther along. *The ice must be drifting southward,* he thought, disappointed, *making our journey much longer.*

CRACKING ICE
AND OPENING LEADS

→

March 29

*T*HE TWO MEN came to an area of tightly packed ice, but the snow hid deep cracks. One team of dogs suddenly disappeared into a hole in the ice, along with the sled. Quickly, the men jumped down and unloaded the gear. They hauled out the supplies, pack by pack, with ropes. Then each dog had to be lifted. The unbroken sled was carefully dragged up and had to be reloaded before they could set off again.

Nansen noticed the weather changing, the temperature rising to a balmy −30°C (−22°F), which they called "pure summer." The two men set off over a trail of good ice with light hearts and a southerly wind at their backs. But again they came to an opening lead and had to scramble to run one sled across. They jumped back as the lead widened rapidly. Johansen managed to jump to the other side, throwing his chest over the ice edge, but dunking his legs in the water.

Cracks and leads in the ice.

Here was a big problem. Nansen and two sleds were on one side of the gap; Johansen, on the opposite side, was stranded and moving away from his partner with the rapid drift of the ice. Johansen's wet clothes quickly froze. To keep warm, he sprinted around the barking dogs, flapping his arms.

The tent and the stove were on Nansen's side of the lead, and the fragile kayaks were riddled with holes. They would be useless until they could be repaired.

Nansen began desperately to search for a way to cross the widening water. He made a long detour and finally found a crossing place but had difficulty on such delicate ice getting his two teams of dogs and sleds over to the other side.

When Nansen reached Johansen, he was amazed to see the ice was flat and easier for travel. Since they had to move rapidly to reach the North Pole in time, Nansen gave orders to push onward. "*Sass,*" he shouted at the dogs.

Johansen followed, his frozen clothes rattling as he walked. He wondered how Nansen could ignore the sound. Johansen's wind pants had torn from his fall, too, and he wanted to get into dry clothes. For a while Johansen kept silent, but when he saw that Nansen had no intention of stopping soon, he spoke up. He said they needed to camp so he could get out of his clothes and mend his wind pants.

Annoyed at possibly losing the rest of the fine day, Nansen shot back, "My God, it's not like we're womenfolk."

Johansen said no more, and they marched on in stony silence until Nansen found a place to pitch the tent. As Johansen took off his trousers caked with ice, he knew he would not forget the way Nansen had been unfair to him.

DESPERATE WORK

April 2–4

NO SOONER HAD they spread out the sleeping bag than Nansen fell asleep, food in hand. In a dream, he walked into a cold dining room with hot dishes steaming on the table, including a beautiful, fat goose. Other guests were arriving, so he went outside to greet them, but stumbled right into deep snow. He heard someone laughing and woke to find himself shivering in a sleeping bag on the drift ice in the far north. Which made him feel absolutely miserable.

Next day, he and Johansen dragged their bodies out of the warm, soggy bag, silently packed their gear, harnessed the dogs, and drove onward all day and into the sunlit night. Johansen wanted to turn around. He wrote in his journal that "we ought not to tempt Fate by continuing much further north."

Northwards through the Drift Snow, April 1895, by H. Egidius based on a photo by Nansen.

With ice floes in motion around them and massive blocks of ice to hurdle, Nansen also wondered if it was really possible to go one inch farther in this icy bedlam.

He looked down at his watch to see it was barely ticking. He checked with Johansen and found that Johansen's watch had completely stopped. The two men had been working so hard the last few hours that they had forgotten to wind their watches. If they did not know the time of day, they could not know exactly where they were on the planet. It would be impossible to use their navigational instruments to tell them their longitude, how far east or west they were. Nansen would have to do his best to figure out where they were by dead reckoning, calculating their position based on previous readings and distances traveled, but this calculation would be complicated by the fast-moving ice carrying them in different directions, often contrary to where they were headed. Keeping at least one watch running at all times was essential.

Nansen climbed a hill of ice and looked out to report: "nothing but ridge after ridge and long stretches of old rubble ice with very deep snow and lanes here and there." The dogs could not work any harder.

Nansen wished he had brought more dogs. Ice debris and open water hindered another day of travel. Slogging beside his sled, Nansen splashed into the water. He managed to grab the back of his sled, and the dogs dug their paws into the ice and dragged the sled and Nansen out. But so much chaos of ice made it impossible to stop or camp, to change clothes and get dry. So for the rest of the day, Nansen wore a "chain mail of ice."

Polar landscape in the spring.

FARTHEST NORTH

→

GAZING NORTHWARD FROM the top of a thirty-foot ridge, Nansen looked out at an impassable mess of frozen blocks stretching to the horizon. Here he decided to travel one final day. *Just possibly,* he thought, *a path might open up.* But he knew this was wishful thinking.

Packed ice on the horizon.

They started out around two in the morning, but even giants would get tired lifting sleds over such treacherous ice. Nansen skied ahead. He climbed the highest hummock, praying he'd find a way forward.

After only four miles, Nansen made the agonizing decision to end his quest for the pole. With Arctic summer fast approaching, they needed sufficient time in the shrinking ice to find land hundreds of miles to the south. It was far from certain that they would succeed at even that. In fact, the islands of Franz Josef Land were now farther away than the pole itself, and the men were dangerously low on food. They would need to hunt for animals soon.

Less than a month out from the *Fram*, with a heavy heart, Nansen's dream to be the first to reach the North Pole was dashed on the impenetrable ice ridges and open leads ahead. This would have to be the spot: 86°14′ N, or 232 nautical miles from the pole. It was the farthest north any human had ever traveled, 174 miles farther than the record set by Greely thirteen years before.

Nansen and Johansen set up their most northerly camp. They raised the Norwegian flag and made the best of their situation with a celebratory meal of pemmican and dried-potato stew, bread and butter, dried chocolate, stewed whortleberries, and hot whey drink. Johansen called it a party. Johansen was happy they were finally turning around.

Northernmost campsite at 86°14′N.

They dove for their sleeping bag. Below was the deep Arctic Ocean, two and a half miles of polar water to the bottom.

Tomorrow they would "bow to the inevitable," turn their "faces in the direction of warmer climes," and return to their families, if they could survive.

Tomorrow they would aim their sights at Cape Fligely, on Rudolf Island, in the archipelago of Franz Josef Land, a small, uncertain target more than three hundred miles away. Tomorrow would also begin the longest and most difficult phase of their epic struggle— another fourteen months trying to stay alive in the high Arctic.

Part Five

TURNING SOUTH

APRIL 8–MAY 31, 1895

Suggen.

Nansen's sketch of Johansen in his sleeping bag.

CALCULATIONS

→

NANSEN AND JOHANSEN woke to a springlike −32°C (−25.6°F) and headed west and south. Amazingly, the ice was smooth enough for skiing. Sometimes it bent like rubber beneath the weight of two men, the dogs, and the sleds.

When another lead started to open up, Nansen ran on skis to jump across. He shouted for the dogs to move quickly. Johansen shoved the sleds from behind. Suggen fell in and had to be rescued, but they had one of their best travel days in a month, making fifteen miles before camping. In high spirits, Nansen and Johansen were actually warm and comfortable inside the tent that now sat in full sunlight, free of hoarfrost, the gray-white crystalline deposit of frozen water vapor that usually formed on the tent ceiling and walls. At last, Johansen could write in his journal without gloves.

Again they made the grave mistake of forgetting to wind their watches. Both clocks had stopped entirely. It was a disaster.

When they realized their mistake, they quickly wound them up, but it was too late. With no real knowledge of their location, Nansen and Johansen would wander the polar ice cap in search of tiny islands.

Polar spring had arrived, and the short Arctic summer was not far behind. When they made camp, they hung their wet clothes on ski poles to dry in full sunshine. This was the first time on their journey that Nansen felt oppressed by the overheated tent sitting in continuous sunlight. The warmer weather, Nansen knew, would soon bring massive amounts of fog and snow.

Nansen studied his observations to figure out where they were. He calculated that indeed they had been drifting north on the pack ice, which was good for the *Fram,* wherever it might be, but not good for two men desperately seeking land to the south. The drift of the ice was slowing their journey to a crawl.

Illustration of
This Inconceivable Toil
by Fridtjof Nansen.

Johansen patched his clothes while Nansen continued to go over geographic calculations. Then they harnessed their dogs, lashed down their gear, and headed out in silence. The temperature rose to −26°C (−15°F). The ice groaned and creaked all around them, and the sound made the dogs uneasy. When Nansen realized he'd left his compass somewhere behind on a hummock and had to go back and search for it, Johansen waited in the sun-frozen solitude. The dogs lay down lifeless, with their heads on their paws in the bright snow. Never before had Johansen felt such an eternal stillness, almost like a paralysis.

The next day was a big one: twenty-five miles! The two men pulled the brims of their hats down over their eyes to guard against the piercing sunlight. One of the sleds ran over both of Johansen's skis and broke them. Nansen also broke a ski. On backup skis now, they had only one spare ski left.

Nansen spotted Arctic fox tracks in the snow and realized they were not alone on the polar ice cap. He wondered what a fox was doing way up here. Did it mean they were close to land? Nansen kept casting his eyes toward the horizon, expecting to see land any moment. His eyes were weary from years of looking at nothing but ice.

A few hours later, their dog Gulen just quit, entirely exhausted. The two men had a special love of Gulen, who had been born on board the *Fram* in December 1893 and who had never known anything in his life but the frozen world of the ice. Johansen carefully placed him on top of his loaded sled. For hours, the big dog did not move even a paw. When Gulen died, only seventeen dogs remained.

Over Difficult Pressure Mounds.

THIN ICE AND BURNING
THE THIRD SLED

April 29

THE SLEDS CAME to a halt in front of a lead where two fast-moving plates of ice collided under the men's feet, suddenly rising up, thundering and crashing.

Johansen raced to retrieve his skis, which he'd left just behind him on the shifting ice. The men scrambled over a towering pressure ridge in motion. At any moment the dogs and sleds could be jammed between the rolling ice blocks.

When they were safe on the other side of a new ridge, the men paused for an extra ration of meat-chocolate. Nansen scanned the ever-widening lead, which was quickly becoming a mini sea, looking for seals' heads breaking the water or a polar bear. Several of the dogs had grown utterly listless. Even one of Nansen's best dogs, Baro, was beginning to show signs of exhaustion. It wouldn't be much longer before he and Johansen would have no dogs to help with the sleds. They had to travel faster.

For days the powerful spring winds moved ice all around, opening lanes in every direction. At lead after lead, they scouted for ways to move forward, sometimes walking four miles in one direction and yet finding no way to cross. They kept hoping for better luck the next day: Perhaps the two sides of a lead might rejoin, or the water would freeze strong enough to pass over. But the warmer late-spring temperatures meant slower freezing times and longer waits. The men needed patience.

Taking a rest on the ice.

It wasn't yet time to mend the rips and holes in the kayaks, because Nansen expected to find land any moment, and anyway these leads were covered in thick skins of ice that could rip the delicate kayaks and make them useless.

At night the ice creaked under their tent. Nansen lay in the bag listening, wondering if they should move before the surrounding towers of ice tumbled down on the tent. Somehow, even in that precarious position, he was able to fall asleep. The terrible sounds of shifting ice made him dream of earthquakes.

On the trail, Nansen staggered and stumbled. One time he just lay there in the snow, longing to stay down, to fall asleep, and to bring a final halt to this mad torture. But again he managed to get up. Hope drove him onward. Land must be just over the horizon.

A few things had started to bother Johansen. First, he resented doing so much of the camp work in the mornings before setting off. Also, he would have to wait outside the tent, ready to go, while Nansen lingered inside over his calculations and his journal.

Nansen's journal at the National Library of Norway, Oslo.

But even more troubling, in two months of travel covering over 350 miles, Johansen had developed a deep frustration with having to drive two sleds and two teams of dogs on the heels of Nansen's one team and one sled. It was true that Johansen was better with the dogs (Nansen tended to get angrier at them), but the men continued to travel without speaking.

They sank to their thighs in loose, deep snow when they took off their skis to better push the sleds. The wind felt like a curse, and a sudden snowstorm created a whiteout. Blindly, they bumped into invisible ice ridges until finally they found a place to camp and sank into their sopping-wet bag like heaps of frozen bones.

When only twelve dogs remained, Nansen finally decided it was time to get rid of the third sled. Johansen thought this should have been done long before, but he was happy about Nansen's decision.

With the wood from the sled, they built their first fire on the trip, just outside the tent door. The tent nearly caught fire. The smoke blinded them, so they quickly moved the fire away from the tent. The fire was so hot it melted a deep hole in the ice.

The men repacked the load of the third sled onto the other two, and now, with six dogs on each sled, off they trekked once more.

We Made Fairly Good Progress.

BIRTHDAY, NARWHALS,
AND BEAR TRACKS

May 15

*J*OHANSEN TURNED TWENTY-EIGHT years old on this day. The men celebrated with pemmican and dried-potato stew, Johansen's favorite, followed by hot lime-juice grog. Nansen proposed a toast to his partner. "To your health, Mr. Johansen. And may you have many a pleasant surprise and happy day in the coming year." As usual, Nansen sounded formal and quite distant for two men who were sharing so much in such close quarters for so long, and who slept in one sleeping bag. But that was Nansen.

One morning on the ice, Nansen heard a strange breathing sound coming from the lead they were about to cross. Johansen had heard the sound, too, but thought it was only the ice floes grinding together in the distance.

Nansen shouted, "Whales!"

Suddenly the water was filled with narwhals! What whales they were, too, each with a tusk five to ten feet long like a spear protruding from the face. Up popped a head, a tusk stabbing the air. One after another, their bodies curled in the water.

Both men ran to the sleds to get their guns, and Nansen set out along a pool of water, ready for a hunt. Heads kept popping up in small openings in the ice, but it would take too much time to stalk one of these shy creatures. Besides, they could not carry any more weight, so they abandoned the idea, trudging onward in a brisk wind and falling snow.

Nansen spotted polar bear tracks. The thought of polar bear steaks made them smile. With the wind behind them, they rigged the sails on the sleds, so the dogs had an easier time pulling.

Nansen's lithograph of a polar bear sniffing at ski tracks.

THE BIRDS COME BACK

May 26

*A*LL DAY THEY trudged toward the water sky, the massive gray blotch above the ice on the horizon that might be a reflection of open water. It was delightful to spot the first bird of spring, a fulmar hovering above one of the kayaks atop the sled.

Nansen's pen-and-ink drawing of gulls in the sea.

After Nansen changed out of his Finn shoes into his lightweight komagers, he felt more nimble on his feet. It was nearly 0°C, or 32°F, almost above freezing, and in another month, with any luck, most of the ice would disappear, and the water would be safe to paddle.

With spring, however, came the pack ice in transition, "this miserable thin young ice . . . utterly treacherous," the lanes and cracks crisscrossing in a nightmare of uneven, loose, irregular ice.

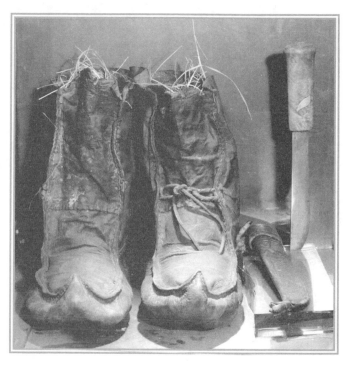

Nansen's komager boots.

Nansen now spotted a black guillemot circling above and heard what sounded like someone blowing on a goat's horn. He cast his eyes to the water. A ringed seal raised its lonely head and then dove below the surface.

The water sky was sharply defined now. He fixed his eyes on the horizon, thirsting for land.

May it be so! thought Nansen.

Part Six

To the

KAYAKS

JUNE 1—JULY 22, 1895

Repairing the Kayaks.

MENDING THE KAYAKS

→

*A*NOTHER MONTH GONE, and still no land. Nansen felt certain June would be different.

Camping at the water's edge, Nansen spotted seals and narwhals near the tent. It was finally time to repair the kayaks. If they could not find land soon, they would have to paddle all the way to Spitsbergen, hundreds of miles on the open sea. They better be ready, thought Nansen. The very idea of being able to paddle on open water eased his constant worry of meeting up with impassable leads.

The remaining six dogs were starving now. It was hard to watch them eat pieces of Johansen's ski, the toe strap and some of the wood edges. One ate her harness.

Rationing their own meals so the remaining provisions might last as long as possible, the two men went without food until their stomachs groaned with pain. Breakfast consisted of a little butter and a tiny piece of bread. Nansen reckoned they had butter for twenty-three days if they could keep it down to about an ounce a day, and bread for thirty-five to forty days. He wondered where they might be in forty days—maybe dead, maybe alive.

Camped in one place, they fixed the frames of the kayaks, then mended and stretched the coverings over the frames to fix the leaks and placed bamboo mesh at the bottom of the boats so the supplies would remain dry when the kayaks shipped water.

The temperature rose above freezing for the first time, to 2°C (35.6°F). The snow was soft, the hummocks dripping in the heat. Drizzle turned to heavy rain, and the men dove for their tent.

Happy that the kayaks were ready to use, they packed the sleds once more to take up their journey in a raging storm that appeared out of nowhere blowing in from the east.

The slushy ice was a foot thick, like walking in freezing oatmeal. Spotting a gull, Nansen dreamed of having wings. Just think how far they could get, and how quickly, if they only had wings!

A small dead codfish floating in a lead reminded Nansen to set out a fishing line the next time they pitched their tent. Later, when he used the dead fish as bait, he caught nothing, and his aching stomach groaned.

WATER SKY, THE COLOR OF HOPE

June 12

WITH ONLY FIVE dogs left, the sleds broke through a thin crust of ice, injuring the dogs' legs. The bitter spring wind soaked into their very bones, and they advanced only a single mile.

In the tent, Nansen was plagued by inner doubts and turmoil, trying to make a decision, simply not knowing if they should push onward or stay where they were to try to capture a seal. Three months after leaving the *Fram*, Nansen thought they had reached "a state of things bad beyond description."

Johansen ducked out of the tent and reported a colossal water sky above the ice to the south. The water sky was their only beacon. "We see it again and again, looking so blue and beautiful; for us it is the color of hope."

When the sun broke out of the "dark, fantastic clouds" the next day, the ever-optimistic Johansen, in contrast to Nansen's gloom, felt it "was strangely beautiful, and we enjoyed it and got into a good mood."

ONE DOG LEFT FOR NANSEN, TWO FOR JOHANSEN

———————————————————————→

June 15

ONLY THREE DOGS remained. Haren and Suggen pulled for Johansen. Kaifas alone worked Nansen's sled.

Nansen went to the front of the sled to join his dog with a special harness that crossed his shoulders like a knapsack and attached to the hauling rope at the belt around his waist, equally distributing weight to his thighs and legs. Dog and man pulled together, but whenever the ice grew the least bit bumpy and the sled came to a halt, Nansen had to go to the back, pushing again, straining all he could to budge the sled forward. Sometimes, with Herculean strength, he lifted the front end of the sled to turn it in a new direction in the heavy snow.

Johansen and his last dog, Suggen, dragging a sledge.

When they got to ridges or lanes, they had to work one sled at a time looking for pathways between hummocks. They inspected their remaining ammunition and found, to their joy, they had 148 shotgun cartridges and 181 rifle cartridges. If they could not get a big animal, at least they had enough ammunition for 148 birds, which, Nansen figured, could keep them alive another three months. *Surely something good will happen in three months!* thought Nansen. He planned also to catch gulls with hooks.

Nansen shot a few fulmars and a guillemot, but missed the seals in the lanes. "How we wished we could get hold of such a prize!"

Even in times of such hardship, Nansen remained a quintessential scientist. When they paused in their travels, he tried to catch small marine animals in the net he had brought for this purpose, but he retrieved little, except for a few crustaceans (tiny shrimplike creatures).

Johansen pulls his sled and kayak.

Hard to believe, but the leads grew worse, a natural consequence of moving south at this time of year. The two men and three dogs started to jump from one small piece of ice to another. Barren winds tore at their tent when they camped. Again the men lay down feeling the hopelessness of their lives. "I lie awake at night by the hour racking my brain to find a way out of our difficulties," Nansen wrote. "Well, well, there will be one eventually!" He was thinking of death.

The west wind brought little auks and the joy of seeing the birds sitting on the waves in couples chattering to themselves. With so much water, it was time to take to the kayaks. No other option existed.

Ice melting in the summer.

SALVATION IS A SEAL

June 21

*T*HEY DREW THE kayaks side by side in the water and placed the skis crosswise to bind them together to make a small catamaran. Then they pushed the sleds on top of the deck, one in front and one in back. The three dogs walked onto the sleds as if they'd done this a million times before. Kaifas and Suggen sat in the bow, and Haren in the stern. With their guns between their knees and all their worldly belongings stuffed inside the kayaks, the men set off on their first real water voyage.

It was difficult to paddle such a makeshift twin kayak contraption with so much stuff on board, but it sure was better than battling the wet snow and slushy ice with the sleds.

Crossing a crack in the ice.

They were enjoying the feeling of freedom, paddling on open water, when suddenly a bearded seal popped to the surface. Johansen grabbed his gun and fired. The seal floated. Nansen harpooned it, and all Nansen's pent-up worry eased. How fortunes could change in an instant.

For breakfast, they feasted on seal liver, seal blubber, and seal soup, and they made seal oil for their lamps from boiling down the blubber.

When they managed to hunt another seal, Nansen decided they should stop paddling for a while and wait for more ice to melt to make kayaking easier. They could live on their catch and their few remaining provisions from the *Fram*.

SEAL-BLOOD PANCAKES
AND TENT ON FIRE

←————————————————————————————

June 24

*T*HEY REMAINED IN one area for a month and called the place "Homesick Camp." Another translation from Norwegian might be "Longing Camp." They longed for the snow to melt to make the ice passable with wider lanes to travel in the kayaks once and for all. They longed for land. They longed for home. When they did speak to each other, the common topic was what it would be like to get back home. As best they could, they avoided being overly irritated with each other. For private time, they took walks alone.

Nansen loved seal blubber either raw or fried. No meat was better than seal meat. For supper, they made pancakes from seal blood, which Johansen said were "first-class."

Johansen was impressed by how much Nansen had learned while living among the Inuit of Greenland. Nansen fashioned an oil-lamp stove for cooking, using a small bowl with a wick made from strips of a canvas bag and some of the bandages they'd brought in their medicine kit.

Cooking in the tent did have a few drawbacks, especially when the heavy smoke from the frying grease got into their eyes, making them tear up and squint in pain. But the worst was the time the blubber and oil from the stove suddenly caught fire. The flames shot up. Nansen grabbed a handful of snow from the floor of the tent and threw it on the stove, which sputtered and crackled and shot even bigger flames to the roof. The men threw their bodies against the entry flap and "dashed headlong into the open air—glad, indeed, to have escaped with our lives."

When they saw their reflections in one of their navigation instruments, they did not recognize the faces staring back at them. Sooty, smoke-smudged, and full-bearded, they looked like barbarians "stirring a mess of soup in a kettle and surrounded on all sides by ice."

They patched the hole in the tent with one of their sails.

It was now exactly two years since the *Fram* had left Kristiania, and 102 days since Johansen and Nansen had left the *Fram*. The warmer month of June had almost passed, but the snow and ice were taking forever to melt.

On a bright Sunday, Nansen was daydreaming of home again, where the world was now in full bloom, "the fjord quivering in the sunlight." He imagined Eva sitting near the water with Liv . . . but then he looked through the tent door at a world of white and was reminded of the many ice floes between where he sat now and his home far away. Adventures like these bring up emotions, good and bad, up and down, like riding a roller coaster.

FIRST BEAR

⟶

July 3

IT STARTED TO rain hard. Nansen prayed it would last for days and melt the rest of the ice so they could once and for all paddle to Svalbard. But the rain turned to snow.

To mend new holes and leaks, the men painted and caulked their kayaks. Nansen created a kind of soot-paint by first burning seal bones, then grating these into a fine powder. He mixed the bone dust with boiled seal blubber, then added more oil and soot. The smoke during this process nearly drove them from the tent. But Nansen kept up his spirits.

One evening, Johansen was glum, knowing he was about to lose Haren, who was a first-rate dog. Johansen looked sadly at the weak animal. It was time for Haren to die, or go, as they put it, "to the happy hunting-grounds, or wherever it may be draught-dogs go to. Perhaps to places where there are plains of level ice and no ridges and lanes."

After Haren was gone, only Suggen and Kaifas were left. The men would have to keep these two alive as long as they could.

Suggen, shortly before he was put down.

Kaifas, shortly before he was put down.

Living almost entirely on their catch now, they also boiled up some hot chocolate left over from the *Fram* supplies to add variety to their meat diet.

Suddenly Kaifas started to bark outside the tent. Nansen jumped up, poked his head outside, and saw a bear run up to the dogs and start sniffing at Kaifas.

Nansen sprang for his gun while the bear glared at him. He put a ball through the bear's chest, "certain that it would drop on the spot." But the bear staggered, then took off running. Nansen fiddled for more cartridges in his pocket as he chased the bear into the hummocks, Johansen following behind.

Nansen thrilled at the chase. For so many weeks, he'd felt nothing but fatigue. Now the hunter's spark was kindled inside him, and his body cleared every obstacle. He was an athlete again.

Wounded badly, the bear could not travel fast, but was fast enough that Nansen had a hard time keeping up over the deep snow and irregular hummocks.

After a long chase, Nansen killed the bear. Kaifas and Suggen were given as much polar bear meat as they could eat, but Suggen was no longer the hearty dog he'd once been. After chasing the bear and gorging himself, he could hardly walk. Johansen put him up on top of his sled, "but then he howled so terrifically, as much as to say it was beneath his dignity to be transported in this way."

DEPARTING HOMESICK CAMP

July 22

*A*FTER A MONTH at Homesick Camp, Nansen couldn't wait any longer for the ice to melt. Summer was almost over. Preparing to leave the camp, Nansen made hard decisions on what equipment to jettison so they could travel light. They tossed out things like rope, a frying pan, some bags, tools, their thick Finn shoes, wolf-skin gloves, a geological hammer, some shirts, and socks, leaving the things scattered on the surface of the snow.

With a few sacks of belongings and some dried seal and bear meat, along with a sixteen-pound pail of bear blubber, they pulled out of Homesick Camp.

Well rested, Kaifas and Suggen had regained their strength.

Part Seven

LAND *at* LAST

JULY 25–AUGUST 15, 1895

Incredibly Slow Progress.

"WE SHALL REACH IT TODAY!"

→

July 25

FROM ATOP A hummock, Johansen spotted a black stripe just above the horizon. It rose on a slant into what seemed like a bank of clouds. Nansen grabbed the telescope to investigate. He fixed his eye on the black part, then realized those were rocks! And not that far away, either! Rocks in a large snowfield or glacier stretching far in a westerly direction. All this time he had expected land to look more like high peaks and glittering glaciers. But this *was* land! Absolutely. Land.

It would be impossible to express the joy and disbelief in making such a discovery, especially by two men so accustomed to disappointment. Rocks, not ice. Now it made sense to Nansen why they had seen so many little auks passing over Homesick Camp. In fact, they had been looking at this sliver of land for a whole month. Many times they had seen this same formation in the distance but had surmised it was simply a different kind of cloud, or perhaps mist.

Nansen hoped to reach the land by next evening, but Johansen said, "We shall reach it today!"

In fact, it would take them fourteen long days, navigating treacherous and disintegrating drift ice. They took off their skis and eagerly dragged their sleds on foot. When it came time to camp, they tried lying on the bare ice in blankets without the tent, but they got chilled because they were so wet from the day's hard work of driving sleds with only one dog each.

Next day Nansen's back was killing him; he summoned every ounce of energy and power to drag himself onward. Johansen led out front and helped Nansen haul his sled over the difficult spots.

Nansen's pain increased until he could barely walk, so Johansen took both sleds across the ice. When they made camp again, Nansen could not even take off his own boots and socks by himself, so Johansen cared for him as if he were a child.

Each day the land looked closer. But when they woke, they discovered the strong winds had blown their drift ice farther away. One day the two dogs fell into the frozen sea and came out looking like frost devils.

A week passed. It seemed they would never reach those rocks.

Nansen's pen-and-ink drawing of a polar bear on the ice during the bear hunt.

POLAR BEAR ATTACK

August 4

NOT YET ON land, Nansen was lifting his sled onto the ice edge of a lead when he heard a scuffle behind him. Johansen, who had been pulling his own sled flush with Nansen's, had been attacked by a polar bear.

The starving animal had followed, then, hiding behind massive ice blocks, waited for the right moment to pounce. It had slinked its way up to the men while they were clearing the ice from the lead, their backs turned. When Johansen stooped down to pick up the hauling rope, he spotted the bear crouched near the end of the kayak. At first he thought it was Suggen.

Before he had time to realize it was not a dog, the bear sprang on Johansen, sending its giant paw across his ear and knocking him flat on his back, making his "bones rattle" in his head.

Lying between the legs of the bear, Johansen grabbed the bear's throat with one hand, holding it fast, clinching with all his might. He defended himself with the fist of his other hand. He saw the bear's jaw gaping over his head "and the terrible teeth glistening." He wanted to grab his gun nearby in the kayak, but the bear was just about to bite his head, and he shouted to Nansen, "Get the gun!"

Nansen struggled for his gun on the foredeck of his kayak. But the kayak began to slip away from the ice into the water. For a split moment, Nansen wondered if he should just jump into the water and fire from over the deck of the kayak, but he worried about getting off a good shot. He didn't want to hit his friend. So with a giant effort, he yanked the kayak, heavy with cargo, right up onto the high edge of the ice. Then he dropped to his knees and tugged at the gun with no time to see what was now happening to his friend behind him.

Meanwhile, the bear turned to look at Nansen, and that short pause was probably what saved Johansen's life.

Johansen shouted again, "Look sharp, or it'll be too late!"

Nansen sat down and cocked his shotgun. The bear caught sight of Suggen and turned toward the dog, which gave Johansen a fleeting moment to let go of the bear's throat and wriggle away.

The bear whacked Suggen on the head, and the dog started to howl. A few yards from Nansen, the bear also went for Kaifas, who was barking wildly. When Nansen shot the bear, the animal fell dead between the two men.

"You must look Sharp!"

The whole event had taken a matter of seconds. Now the water lapped softly against the kayak. A dog whined. The bear had scraped some grime off Johansen's right cheek, leaving a white stripe on his face and an open wound on one of his hands. Kaifas had escaped with only a scratch to the nose.

The two men fed as much raw polar bear meat to the dogs as they could eat. They cut up thin slices and placed them on the snow to cool, then ate them happily until they, too, were stuffed.

Stowing as much meat as they could pack into the kayaks and some bear fat for fuel, they ferried across the lead on their way toward the ever-receding land. They harnessed themselves to the sleds and waded through ponds of ice water, sinking to their thighs, their boots gurgling, the frozen slush spraying up on all sides. They hardly noticed the bear tracks everywhere, crisscrossing the wet snow.

We Reach Open Water, August 6, 1895.

FOLLOWING ALONG GLACIERS

August 6

NANSEN HEARD THE breakers pounding, then spotted open water—the Arctic Ocean. Behind the dark surface of the wide sea, glaciers loomed in the distance. Joy pumped through Nansen's heart. His back was much better now, and he waved his hat to Johansen far behind him. The faint cry of his partner sang out in the wind, "Hurrah!"

To celebrate, they paused for a chunk of chocolate. They rigged their kayaks at the edge of the open sea. Because it was not yet safe to leave the sleds behind, Nansen again lashed the kayaks together and ran the sleds up top.

Nansen's last dog, Kaifas.

Sadly, though, it was now time to part with the last two dogs. Johansen and Nansen loved their sled dogs, who were survivors like themselves, who had faithfully accompanied them through all their human trials. But there was simply no room for dogs on the wider sea. To make these final deaths somewhat bearable, each man took his companion's favorite dog behind a hummock to send it to the "happy hunting grounds."

Putting thoughts of their dogs behind them, the men pushed off from the edge of the floe, and the double kayak danced over the water. Nansen was thrilled to be on the open sea for the first time in two years. Even the wind was with them, so they rigged a sail and glided effortlessly through heavy mist along a massive glacier that rose straight up from the sea in front of them. They paddled along a wall of ice sixty feet high, and the glacier made booms like cannon shots when large chunks of ice broke loose and tumbled into the sea.

A seagull on the sledge.

Finding a place to camp was not easy. They had to set up their tent on a drifting floe with high hopes of reaching solid land the following day. When they woke surrounded by ice, their spirits sank. The ice pack had trapped them once more. Unwilling to surrender, they hauled their gear to open water and again rigged up the double kayak. It was a beautiful paddle through a cold mist that slowly burned away and left the sea a perfect mirror with bits of ice floating by.

All around them were uncharted islands of different sizes. Nansen named two of them. The first he called "Eva's Island"; the second, "Liv's Island." (Later these islands were discovered to be two halves of just one island, now called Eva-Liv Island.)

ROGUE WALRUS

August 11

SUDDENLY A WALRUS "raised itself high out of the water, snorted so that the air shook," then dove and quickly appeared on the opposite side near Johansen. The men jammed their paddles into the water to frighten it away. Johansen fired his gun, and "it uttered a terrific bellow, rolled over, and disappeared."

Pastel sketch of a walrus by Fridtjof Nansen, 1893.

The two men paddled as fast as they could, until suddenly, Johansen's kayak jumped into the air. Even with a bullet in its forehead, the walrus was attacking. Nansen shot it again, and this time it floated in the water, dead. Gulls whirled overhead. The men carved meat and blubber off its carcass. When one of their knives punctured a lung, it quickly filled with water, making the animal so heavy they had to let it sink "in circles towards the bottom, while the gulls made a terrible row because they had been cheated of a share in the catch."

When the fog lifted, the men saw land stretching out before them to the south and west, a chain of islands covered in glaciers, and for the first time in two years, they pulled their boats onto shore.

FEET ON DRY LAND

August 15

AT LAST THEY touched bare land with their feet. They marveled at the moss and beautiful Arctic poppies growing among the stones. Like boys, they jumped from granite block to granite block, then sat apart from each other with their feet lovingly kicking the ground, overwhelmed by private thoughts.

They ran up the Norwegian flag and prepared a feast cooked over their seal-oil lamp. They sat inside the floorless tent with big grins on their faces, kicking granite sand instead of snow. To sleep on dry land with no icy puddles of water underneath them seemed like a miracle.

Part Eight

FRANZ JOSEF LAND

BEARS, WALRUS, AND A WINTER HOME

AUGUST 16—SEPTEMBER 30, 1895

Camping on the coast of Franz Josef Land.

BUT WHAT LAND?

→

*T*HE SUN BURST from the puffy clouds. The beach was covered in shells, and the water was full of snails and sea urchins. The nearby cliff was home to hundreds of screaming little auks. Fluttering snow buntings kept the men in a cheerful mood.

Taking a reading with their sextant, they knew they were at 81°27′ north latitude, but the longitude? How far east or west? Nansen kept tumbling geography over and over in his brain, still unable to get his bearings, despite Julius Payer's maps and descriptions from the *Tegetthoff* Expedition of 1874.

When they climbed the cliff to take photos of the black-backed gulls breeding in the rocks, they looked out at miles of drift ice stretching to the horizon from where they'd come. Nansen thought of the *Fram* and their comrades out there still frozen solid in the ice. He spotted other craggy islands and open leads in the direction they wanted to go.

Knowing it was not quite time to settle down for the winter, they packed up, got back in the kayaks, and moved farther south. They had to put more miles behind them if they expected to make it to Spitsbergen before winter. They paddled into a thin layer of new ice. As the wind stiffened, they set their sails and followed the glacier all night long, eating a meal of cold boiled bear and a few ounces of bread.

COLD CLOSING IN, TIME TO WINTER OVER

August 26

A SOUTHWEST WIND drove more ice upon them, blotting out the open sea, and packing in so tightly against the coast they could see nothing "but piled-up ridges, hummocks, and broken ice in all directions." They threw their sleeping bag down on the ice and put the tent over them to sleep. As the floe continued to pack and shift and rumble all around them, it began to snow heavily. Nansen was now sure they would not reach Norway this year. The best they might do was to reach the south coast of the archipelago, maybe even Eira Harbor, where they might find the abandoned storage hut of British explorer Benjamin Leigh Smith.

The *Tegetthoff* Expedition had previously discovered, mapped, and named Franz Josef Land. Then in 1880 and 1881, in a steamer called the *Eira*, Leigh Smith made additional charts of Franz Josef Land. On his first journey north, he collected valuable Arctic specimens, including two polar bear cubs. The following year, he found a harbor and named it after his ship, then built a storehouse, which he packed with supplies, and was ready to search for the lost ship *Jeannette*. But when he set off, his steamer was nipped and crushed in the ice at nearby Cape Flora on Northbrook Island. He and his crew survived there for ten months before returning home in four boats they could sail southward through open leads.

The last tent site before building the winter cabin.

Nansen and Johansen traveled for many days on fast-moving ice floes buffeted about by strong winds that nearly tipped them over. When the seas were too rough to launch their fragile kayaks, they submitted to drifting with the ice. When they got closer to land, they explored islands and edges of glaciers until, finally realizing Eira Harbor and Leigh Smith's hut were just too far away to reach before freeze-up, Nansen decided it was time to settle down for the long polar night.

Late in August, the men found a good, flat spot on a nameless island near some cliffs that led to an inland glacier. At the base of the cliff were plenty of stones for building a winter den. Lots of bear tracks meant a good source of meat and clothing for the cold, dark months ahead.

HARVESTING WALRUS FOR WINTER

August 29

*O*UT ON THE ice, herds of walrus bellowed day and night. Overhead, geese honked their way southward, causing pangs of homesickness in Nansen's heart.

To prepare for winter, the two men hunted walrus. Again, they lashed the kayaks together for stability, and with their guns and harpoons at the ready, they paddled out for walrus battle. One time, forgetting his gun was cocked, Nansen threw it into its case on deck so he could paddle faster, and the loaded gun went off. The ball passed through the deck and out the side right above the waterline, just missing one of his legs.

Coming upon a group of dozing walrus on the shore ice, Nansen looked into the sad eyes of one of the dying animals that he had shot and was moved. In spite of its vast, shapeless, and what he considered almost demonic-looking body, he had feelings for the creature. He said, "There was something so gently supplicating and helpless in its round eyes as it lay there that its goblin exterior and one's own need were forgotten in pity for it. It almost seemed like murder." Those walrus eyes would haunt him for years, for "it seemed as if in them lay the prayer for existence of the whole helpless walrus race."

Of course, Nansen knew it was a matter of survival for him and Johansen. They had to have meat to get through the winter, and also enough hides to build their shelter. So the two explorers put away their sadness and rejoiced at all the meat and blubber they could now store for the dark months.

One problem, however, was getting the heavy animals skinned, cut up, and hauled back to camp. It was no easy task. Some of the adult walrus males weighed over two tons. One particularly foul-weather day, they got caught skinning a walrus out on an ice floe that broke free and started to move out to sea. Luckily, they had their kayaks, but could make little headway against the fierce wind and towering waves, spume flying everywhere. They paddled like madmen through a choppy sea, fighting to hold on to their paddles with aching arms. The wind almost lifted the light boats into the air. The kayaks listed to one side with the heavy weight of a walrus skin, which they had to let go, or capsize. The screaming gulls at once attacked the floating treasure.

A Fight Against the Storm to Reach Land, August 29, 1895.

Finally, Nansen and Johansen clambered ashore. They were soaked and chilled to the bone, but felt safe and snug in their tent. "A good potful of meat was prepared, and our appetite was ravenous. It was, indeed, with sorrow that we thought of the lost walruses now drifting out there in the storm."

BUILDING A WINTER DWELLING

September 3

SOON ALL THE BIRDS would head south, the sun would sink out of sight, and the sea would close permanently with thick winter ice in the polar night that was about to engulf them with its unbroken silence.

Nansen and Johansen worked hard collecting stones from the base of the cliff. They dug a hole for their hut and began to build walls. Mostly they used their bare and frozen hands, but they also fashioned a spade by tying the shoulder blade of a walrus to a broken ski. For a pickax, they attached a walrus tusk to a wooden piece of a sled.

For weeks, they worked in falling snow. Gradually, the three-foot walls rose above the internal floor three feet below the surface. Now they set about making the roof out of walrus hides hung over a ridgepole fashioned from a large log. The colossal walrus hides were frozen and extremely heavy, and had to be rolled and dragged up from the shore. Then they were soaked in seawater to make them pliable, stretched over the top of the hut, and held in place with stones at the ends attached by strips of hide.

Walrus.

The men laid in as much meat and fuel as they could stockpile for the winter and stored a supply of walrus blubber and bear meat on the roof of the hut, covered over by polar bear skins.

Actually, calling this a hut sounds too cozy. It was an icy, cold hole in the ground. A "creep-in" might be a better way to describe the dwelling, which was only ten feet long and six feet wide. Lying down, the men touched the wall with their feet. Nansen could not quite stand up straight without bumping his head on the roof. He was delighted, nevertheless, that for the first time since leaving the *Fram*, they had shelter from the harsh wind where they actually could stretch their limbs a little!

A door in one corner led to a short tunnel to the outside, the openings at each end covered with bearskin curtains. This passage was so low and tight they had to creep through it in a squatting posture. Nansen was taller and had the most difficulty getting in and out.

They made beds of stone and tried sleeping apart for the first time in months, but they woke so frozen that no amount of "blubber and boiling-hot bear-soup" could warm them, so they sewed blankets together to make one sleeping bag again and slept side by side for the rest of winter.

As the days passed, they boiled and roasted their meals in one corner of their new home that became a kitchen. They cut a round hole in the walrus-hide roof and made a smoke-board out of polar bear skins to guide the smoke up to the hole. They built a chimney of ice and snow on the roof to create a good updraft and keep the wind from blowing the smoke back down into the hut.

The men buried a few provisions left over from the *Fram* and covered them with stones to save them for traveling next spring. And then they settled into the polar night in this raw, cold stone den, like hibernating bears. Sometimes in their stone shelter, they slept for days at a time, waiting and longing for the spring, when they could move southward again.

Part Nine

POLAR NIGHT

OCTOBER 1–DECEMBER 31, 1895

Snow-covered winter.

BEAR-MEAT SOUP
AND BLUBBER CAKES

→

October 1

FOR THE NEXT nine months, Nansen and Johansen fought off the effects of prolonged hibernation. The monotony and extended silences made their brains dull. What conversations they did have repeated themselves.

At least they had stored enough food for the winter; they were well stocked in polar bear legs, shoulders, and whole carcasses buried in the snow around the hut. They never tired of the menu: bear-meat soup in the morning and fried bear steaks in the evening. They always seemed to be hungry. One specialty they made was to turn the bear's stomach inside out, fill it with blood, then freeze it into a solid mass before cutting it up into pieces to fry in a pan! They both agreed, however, that the best part of the bear was its brain, which they also fried.

THIEVING FOXES

October 15

*T*HE TWO MEN saw the sun for the last time that year, as the bears came to gnaw on the meat and blubber on the roof of the hut. Nansen woke to the sounds of rummaging outside. He crawled through the entrance tunnel, but saw nothing in the moonlight. The ghost bears had vanished.

Foxes raided their camp and stole anything they could carry away. Nansen kept several things in a marine specimen net hidden near a big stone, but the curious foxes found it. From the net, they stole pieces of bamboo, steel wire, and harpoon line, and a collection of rocks that Nansen had brought from the first bare land they'd encountered. The foxes also went off with a large ball of twine to play with, which Nansen had kept to make thread for clothes, shoes, and a new sleeping bag.

One day a fox dragged a thermometer into the snow. The men found it, brought it back, and covered the instrument with stones. The foxes moved the stones and took it once again. The third time, the foxes stole it for good. One particularly ambitious fox dragged off one of their kayak sails, which they would need on their voyage across open water to Spitsbergen in the spring. Johansen found it onshore.

The foxes scurried around on the roof and walked around the men's winter lair like domestic dogs, gnawing on the leftover bones of bears. Nansen and Johansen did not mind this, though; they had plenty of meat to share.

DWELLING COMFORT

→

November 21

DAYS PASSED WITHOUT either man stepping outside except to go to the bathroom or fetch freshwater ice, which they melted in a pot over one of the lamps for drinking water. They also had to collect seawater for sealing openings and cracks in the walls of the hut. The simplest activities outside made them ravenously hungry.

In spite of everything, they were moderately comfortable in their winter home. They tried to keep the temperature above freezing with the seal oil lamps burning night and day. Over by the walls, however, the damp air formed frost crystals on the stones. Sometimes Nansen imagined these frozen walls were marble hallways. When the temperature inside the dwelling rose, the ice on the walls melted and ran down into their sleeping bag.

IDLE ARCTIC DAYS AND NIGHTS

→

November 27

EACH WEEK NANSEN and Johansen took turns cooking. This was one of the variations of their dull lives that gave them a sense of schedule. It broke up the time as they reckoned how many more weeks each had as cook before spring would come.

The cook had to keep the lamps burning. The cook was also the waiter. The two men crept into their bag and brought out their tin cups, while the cook fished up pieces of bear from the pot. They ate with their fingers, then they gulped down the broth.

Polar bear.

Nansen had planned to accomplish a lot during the winter. He wanted to work on his notes and geographical observations. He planned to spin out tales from the journey. But in fact, he accomplished little. It was not the weak light of the lamp that stopped him or the discomfort of working in such a cramped space on hard stones. It was simply that this caveman existence made it almost impossible for him to work.

LEADEN DARKNESS OUTSIDE

→

December 1

ONE DAY NANSEN stepped out of the stone lair into a spectral gray world. The snow boxed his ears. Gusts of wind roared through the cracks and holes of the basalt cliff behind the hut. He spied the eerie forms of black stones in the snow along the beach. He turned his head out to sea to find the same leaden darkness everywhere. Inside or outside the hut, he felt completely shut off from the world, locked inside himself.

Needing exercise, the two men ran sprints up and down the shore like Arctic ghosts. Some nights when Nansen took walks outside, the moon turned the ice world into a fairyland. He wrote:

The hut is still in shadow under the mountain which hangs above it, dark and lowering; but the moonlight floats over ice and fjord, and is cast back glittering from every snowy ridge and hill. A weird beauty, without feeling, as though of a dead planet, built of shining white marble. . . . and now as ever the moon sails silently and slowly on her endless course through the lifeless space. And everything so still, so awfully still, with the silence that shall one day reign when the earth again becomes desolate and empty, when the fox will no more haunt these moraines, when the bear will no longer wander about on the ice out there, when even the wind will not rage—infinite silence!

Nansen called on deep reserves of patience he hardly knew he possessed. He kept telling himself that "spring will come, the fairest spring that earth can give us." But, for the time being, the snow blew hard. He had to be content with his fortune, lying in the cold, cramped quarters of the stone hut, eating polar bear steak, and listening to the wind seethe overhead.

One cloudless morning, Nansen stepped outside to see shooting stars, some with trails of shining dust.

To prepare for Christmas, they scraped the ashes out of the hearth, threw out all the old bones and scraps of meat on the floor, and broke up the thick ice that was making the floor higher and the hut roof lower. When they stepped outside again, they were dazzled by the dancing rainbow colors of the northern lights.

Ink drawing by Nansen of a hiker under the northern lights.

CHRISTMAS
AND
NEW YEAR'S EVE

————————————————————————————→

December 21

A T MIDDAY ON the winter solstice, a faint glimmer of light emanated from the south. From this day on, the sun would begin its journey north again, until it would finally appear on the horizon on March 16.

They had scarcely been able to wash at all, covered as they were in grease, soot, sweat, blood, and grime. The few clothes they possessed had turned to filthy rags and stuck to their foul skin.

To celebrate Christmas Eve a few days after the solstice, Nansen and Johansen turned their shirts inside out, only a slight improvement. Johansen cut his hair. Nansen changed into his second pair of grimy underpants after he bathed with a quarter cup of warm water, using his discarded underwear for a towel. He felt renewed whenever his clothes did not stick to his body quite as much.

The fierce wind made it drafty inside the hut. Nansen had never spent such a desolate Christmas Eve. They allowed them-selves to dig up some of the few precious supplies remaining from the *Fram* and feasted on powdered fish-and-maize flour with oil. For dessert, they fried bread in bear's blubber.

The winter cabin on New Year's Eve night.

December 25

They saved the chocolate for Christmas, a windless day, bathed in beautiful moonlight, solemn and deeply peaceful. When the two men stepped outside, the heavens blazed with northern lights, a pale yellow bow arcing in the southern sky. Streamers of light "flickered and blazed . . . whirled round like a whirlwind . . . darted backward and forward, now red and reddish-violet, now yellow, green, and dazzling white. . . . and then it all became one whirling mass of fire up there . . . a whirlpool of fire in red, yellow, and green."

On New Year's Eve, another year came to an end as the wind howled over glaciers and snowfields, and swept down upon them from the crest of the mountain behind.

On the very last night of 1895, after so many months of sharing the same sleeping bag to stay warm, Nansen was in a generous and friendly mood. The reserved and stately Fridtjof Nansen turned to Hjalmar Johansen and proposed that from now on his companion could use the familiar "you" instead of "thou," the formal address that Johansen had used when speaking to the scientist ever since they first met more than three years ago.

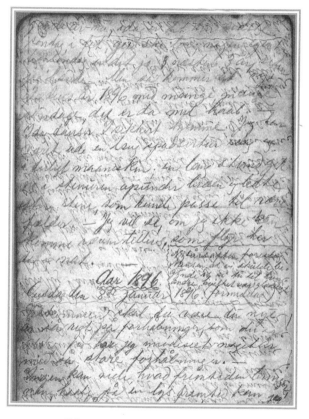

Johansen's journal, January 1, 1896.

Even though the two men would continue to call each other Mr. Nansen and Mr. Johansen, by allowing his companion to use the informal "you," Nansen showed a real sign of growing familiarity.

Part Ten

PREPARING
to MOVE AGAIN
JANUARY 1–MAY 18, 1896

The sledges prepared for travel.

THE TROMSØ SLOOP

→

January 1, 1896

*T*HE NEW YEAR began at −41.5°C (−43°F) with frostbitten fingertips and dazzling moonlight. It was so cold the glacier above them boomed like the sound of an exploding cannon. The sky and the earth trembled. Nansen felt the ground quake even when he slept.

The weather was furious. When Nansen stuck his head outside, the icy wind took his breath away. He lay awake many sleepless nights, turning from side to side on the rough stones, kicking his feet back and forth to drive a little warmth into them. The more he wanted to sleep, the harder it was to fall sleep.

On January 8, Nansen's daughter, Liv, turned three years old, and he hardly knew her. She'd been such a little thing when he set out on his great North Pole journey. Next birthday Nansen hoped they'd be together and become great friends. He would tell her stories about the north and Arctic bears, foxes, walruses, and other strange animals that lived on the ice.

Nansen had to stop thinking of his girl. It was too painful.

What would it really be like to return to Norway? This continued to be the main topic of the limited conversations between the two men. They speculated on how far the *Fram* might have drifted while they had been away. They worried the ship might reach Norway before them. They convinced themselves they would be home by July and that the *Fram* could not possibly get out of the pack ice in time to reach home before autumn. Nansen badly wanted to beat the ship back to Norway, because if it happened the other way round, his family and friends would surely think he and Johansen had died.

Nansen's drawing of Life in Our Hut.

Whenever they needed to boost their spirits, they pictured themselves paddling up to an imaginary whaling sloop they called the "Tromsø sloop," which would rescue them and surround them instantly in great luxury—clothes, sugar, bread, and butter. (Tromsø is a large town in Norway north of the Arctic Circle and a jumping-off point for expeditions and sealers. The *Fram* had harbored there on its way to the Siberian coast.)

Just wait until we get on that Tromsø sloop, they told each other, where there would be all the books they could ever read. They pictured new, soft woolen clothes, from which they could pick out anything they wanted. They dreamed of a Turkish bath.

When they moved around the hut, the skin inside their thighs was raw and bleeding. Trying to keep dirt out of the sores, Nansen washed them with moss or a rag he made from one of the medicine kit bandages.

Their beards grew long; their hair fell shaggy over their shoulders, which helped keep them warm. Their faces were blackened by soot, with only the whites of their teeth and eyes showing in the light of the fire.

Each man had his darker moments. Johansen would grow depressed thinking about "spending the best days of one's life up here." He wrote in his journal that "Monotony has told on both of us. . . . If we did not have the certainty of returning to the world, this existence would be unbearable."

Considering their different backgrounds and personalities, however, they got along amazingly well for two men cooped up in a tiny stone hovel for nine months. Certainly there were tensions. One day Nansen noticed Johansen looking more agitated than usual. In fact, he looked out of sorts. Finally, Johansen turned to Nansen and said there was one thing that really bothered him, and he could not get it out of his mind. It was that time on their way north a year ago, when the floes were separating, and Johansen had fallen into the water, and his ripped wind pants turned to ice. Nansen had wanted to keep going, and not camp to let Johansen change into dry clothes. And when Johansen said it was time to camp, Nansen had called his manliness into question.

"I did not deserve that," Johansen blurted out.

Surprisingly, Nansen agreed that his steadfast partner had indeed not deserved to be treated like that. Nansen admitted he had been thinking only of his own drive to keep going, to reach the pole in what limited time they had. Nansen would later say that for years to come he regretted his own indifference.

As the precious light of spring returned to the sky and the temperature outside slowly rose, the two men felt amazingly healthy—except for a solid two weeks when Nansen's back again was in such pain he lay in bed day and night while the kind and caring Johansen did all the cooking and nursing.

Nansen's back got better, and all their thoughts turned to travel.

THE RETURN OF BEARS

March 16

*T*HE SUN APPEARED, a sliver of light on the horizon for the first time in six months. The birds arrived with the cheerful twittering of little auks. *Blessed birds*, thought Nansen. *How welcome you are!*

Johansen celebrated the return of the sun by scurrying on all fours up the steep debris pile and across a few small glaciers to the top of the mountain behind. The view was spectacular—fjords, ice, glaciers stretching out forever in the brilliant sunlight. The "velvet-like and stately" little auks flew all around him.

The first bear of spring showed up in the nick of time. The men were low on food again. It was Johansen's week for cooking. He lifted the curtain over the inner door and quickly tumbled backward, yelling out, "There's a bear standing just outside the door."

The bear wanted to come into the hut. Johansen again lifted the door cover, aimed his gun, and fired blindly into the passageway. With a dull growl, the bear darted away and scurried up the pile of rocks behind the hut. Nansen chased it down, and for six weeks they lived on that bear.

Nansen's drawing of Johansen Firing Through the Opening.

FINAL PREPARATIONS
FOR THE JOURNEY SOUTH

April 20

THERE WAS MUCH to do before their journey south. They made new clothes out of blankets. They patched their wind pants and coats, and made new socks and gloves out of bearskin. They repaired their moccasins with new soles from walrus hides using thread from the cotton canvas of the provision bags.

When Johansen tried on his new clothes, he felt quite proud of the way he looked. He said he would keep his new coat for arriving in Norway. He did not want to look like a pirate when he got home.

Nansen ready to head south after nine months in the winter cabin.

Johansen ready to head south.

The ivory gulls increased in number through April. Burgomaster gulls drummed at the roof and pecked at the discarded bones of bears around the hut. Then polar bears grew more and more pesky. Whenever the men heard heavy footsteps approaching, they instinctively snatched their guns and dove into the bright April sunshine that stung their eyes. They packed fresh polar bear meat and blubber into the fuel canisters.

Their first tent had been torn to shreds long ago, and the foxes had chewed the remains of it to bits. So now they planned to make a tent from raised sleds and kayaks positioned around them. They would lay their skis and ski poles across the outside and spread the sails over it all. This, Nansen figured, would be an effective shelter. He would plug the cracks and openings with their extra clothes.

The most essential items to bring were their firearms, which each man had kept in good working order. They cleaned their rifles one last time, rubbed them with oil, put Vaseline and gun oil on the locks. Nansen counted the remaining ammunition and was overjoyed to find that they still had 100 rifle cartridges along with 110 small-shot cartridges, enough, he thought, if necessary, for several more winters.

Part Eleven

The

JOURNEY SOUTHWARD

MAY 19—JUNE 16, 1896

DEPARTURE AND A NOTE

→

*T*HE ADVENTURERS LOADED and lashed down their gear and kayaks onto the two sleds. Before leaving, they ducked into the lair one last time to take a photo of themselves. Nansen also composed a note that outlined their journey and stuffed it into a brass tube. He plugged it with a piece of wood and hung it from the driftwood ridgepole in the roof. The note read:

Tuesday, May 19, 1896. *We were frozen in north of Kotelnoi at about 78°43′ north latitude, September 22, 1893. Drifted northwestward during the following year, as we had expected to do. Johansen and I left the* Fram, *March 14, 1895, at about 84°4′ north latitude and 103° east longitude, to push on northward. The command of the remainder of the expedition was transferred to Sverdrup. Found no land northward. On April 6, 1895, we had to turn back at 86°14′ north latitude and about 95° east longitude, the ice having become impassable. Shaped our course for Cape Fligely; but our watches having stopped, we did not know our longitude with certainty, and arrived on August 6, 1895, at* *four glacier-covered islands to the north of this line of islands, at about 81°30' north latitude, and about 7°E. of this place. Reached this place August 26, 1895, and thought it safest to winter here. Lived on bear's flesh. Are starting to-day southwestward along the land, intending to cross over to Spitsbergen at the nearest point. We conjecture that we are on Gillies Land.**

Fridtjof Nansen

That evening they left their winter den behind. Although they were overjoyed to be trekking again and homeward bound, they had gotten badly out of shape from lack of exercise, so they tired quickly and camped after only two hours. Their muscles, Nansen knew, would grow stronger with time.

Johansen resting between sledges.

---

* They did not know they had spent the winter in the archipelago of Franz Josef Land. Gillies, or Giles Land, lies between Svalbard and Franz Josef Land, so they thought their paddle in the open sea to Svalbard would be much shorter than it turned out to be.

As they traveled, Nansen carefully studied the land, comparing it with his knowledge of the maps of Benjamin Leigh Smith and Julius Payer. Still, he had no recognition of where they were exactly.

Nansen and Johansen hauling the camp south.

Sails up on the ice in Franz Josef Land.

NEAR DISASTER

OME DAYS, THE men traveled far apart from each other. Big cracks were hidden under fresh snow, and suddenly Nansen fell into one of them. He lay in slushy water, one of his skis caught, unable to move his leg. Fortunately, in the act of falling, he had held his position with a ski pole poking into the ice on the far end of the crack. Clinging tightly to the pole, he waited for Johansen to pull him out.

After a while his staff gave way. The water started creeping up his body. At risk of getting hypothermia (a medical emergency when your body temperature gets too low), he called out. No answer. Then he shouted for help. Louder. Suddenly, in the nick of time, he heard a distant "hullo." The water had risen to his chest, and he was just about to go under when Johansen arrived at the edge of the crack and yanked Nansen out by his jersey.

From then on, both men were careful not to lash their skis too tightly to their feet on such dangerous ice.

When they reached open water, they put the sleds on top and launched their kayaks, freshly caulked at the seams. "It was strange to be using paddles again and to see the water swarming with birds— auks and little auks and kittiwakes all round." They were surprised to see eider ducks and geese, too, and felt happy they'd reached "more civilized" regions.

Sailing in the kayaks.

They hugged the foggy land, which meant changing back to the sleds to travel the ice from time to time. To go faster, they put the sails on the sleds. The sailing sleds were not easy to steer. They lashed an oar on the back of one kayak and a bamboo pole on the other. Then they stood on skis in front of the kayaks as the wind filled the sails, and off they flew full speed.

A LIFE-OR-DEATH SWIM

*A*T LAST THEY heard a sound that lifted their spirits: the crash of breakers. Climbing a hummock, Nansen saw big blue water spread out before them. When they launched their kayaks, they sailed soaking wet in the brisk wind and wild waves crashing over them. They did not care how cold or wet they were. With this open water, they could now attempt the long paddle to Spitsbergen.

This is a staged photo of Nansen and Johansen paddling.
Nansen's camera was damaged with water after a walrus attack on June 15, 1896.

That evening to stretch their legs, stiff from paddling, they pulled over to the edge of the ice so they could climb another hummock to view the scene around them. Nansen had moored the double kayak with a rope made from a raw walrus hide that ran to a ski pole thrust into the ice.

As they explored the area, Johansen looked back at the kayaks and cried, "The kayaks are adrift!"

The men ran as hard as they could, but the boats were moving rapidly out to sea. Without the kayaks, they would die.

Nansen ripped off some of his clothes and shouted, "Here, take my watch!" Then he sprang into the freezing water, swimming as hard as he could. Everything they needed to survive was in the boats. Food, ammunition, guns, clothes. "If he couldn't save the boats, it did not matter" if he cramped and sank.

He summoned all his determination and physical effort. When he began to tire, he turned over to swim on his back and saw Johansen anxiously pacing up and down the ice, unable to help in any way.

Nansen turned over to swim again and saw he was getting closer to the boats. His courage rose inside him. He pushed harder, but he also felt his limbs stiffening and losing all feeling. He knew he was moments away from freezing up. . . . He just had to hold out a moment longer.

Nansen pumped his arms through the icy water, but they grew feeble in spite of what his mind told them to do.

Staged photo of Nansen and Johansen paddling.

He was so close. He believed he could reach the boats; then, as if by a miracle, he managed to stretch out his hand and latch onto a ski lying across the stern. He yanked his limp body to the edge of the kayak, but he could not pull himself up onto the boat yet. He was too weak, stiff, and cold.

He paused, then summoning his last ounce of energy, with a colossal effort, he swung one leg onto the edge of the boat and tumbled up onto the deck.

I Managed to Swing One Leg Up.

He sat there so cold and stiff he could hardly paddle, but he had control. He stood up. He took two strokes of the paddle on one side, then stepped across into the other kayak and did the same from the other side, back and forth, back and forth, to keep the vessel on a straight path. Slowly he guided the craft toward the edge of the ice.

Gusts of wind seemed to pass right through him. He felt utterly numb. His teeth chattered, and he shivered. But he could still use the paddle, and he knew he would get warm when he got back to Johansen.

That was when he spied two auks near the bow. *How good they would be for supper,* he thought. So he drew his shotgun from the cockpit and shot both of them with one discharge. Johansen saw him paddle over to pick up the birds.

When Nansen got to the ice, Johansen jumped into the kayak. Exhausted and shaking, Nansen could scarcely stand. He looked pale, his long hair and beard sopping wet. He was even foaming at the mouth. All he could say was "so cold, so cold."

Johansen ripped off Nansen's wet clothes. He took off his own trousers and put them on Nansen. Then he spread the sleeping bag onto the ice, guided Nansen inside the bag, and covered him with the sail and everything he could find to keep out the cold air.

Nansen's numb feet were frozen as icicles. He lay there in the bag trying to get warm while Johansen, in his underwear, put up the tent and prepared an auk supper. Occasionally, Johansen went over to the sleeping bag, where Nansen was still shaking, and he quietly listened for Nansen's breathing. Even though he, too, was starting to feel cold, Johansen did not want to climb in and disturb his partner as he slowly came back to life inside the bag.

When Nansen finally woke, Johansen asked how he was feeling. Nansen spoke normally for the first time. The hot auk soup soon took away the shock of the cold swim, and they talked about how lucky they were.

The next day his clothes were dry.

It Gazed Wickedly at Us.

WALRUS REVENGE

→

June 15

NANSEN AND JOHANSEN paddled up to the largest herd of walrus they had ever seen, more than two hundred sitting on the ice, lowing like cows, with many more diving and snorting in the open water nearby. Their kayaks glided quickly through a thick mist. Johansen pulled over to the ice for safety, but Nansen kept paddling. With no warning, a walrus rose out of the water, pumped itself onto the edge of Nansen's kayak, and with one flipper, grabbed the other side of Nansen's deck and rammed its six-foot tusks straight through the boat.

It Tried to Upset Me.

Nansen held on tight as he hit the walrus with his paddle as hard as he could. The kayak tilted, so it was almost underwater. As quickly as it had appeared, the walrus dropped into the deep, and when Nansen looked down, he saw water flooding into his boat. He paddled like mad to the edge of the ice, where Johansen helped heave the waterlogged craft to safety. All Nansen's possessions were floating inside the kayak.

To patch the kayak, they camped on the ice, keeping wary eyes on nearby walrus that stared back at them, "grunting and blowing, and now and then clambering up on the edge of the ice, as though they wanted to drive us away."

Part Twelve

RESCUE

CAPE FLORA, NORTHBROOK ISLAND

JUNE 17, 1896

A SOUND LIKE
THE BARK OF A DOG

→

June 17

ANSEN WAS COOK that day. To get breakfast going, he fetched salt water while Johansen slept. He started the stove and dropped meat into the pot. Before he jumped back into the bag to let the food simmer, he noticed yesterday's mist was lifting, so he decided to climb a nearby hummock and have a look around.

A gentle offshore breeze carried "the confused noise of thousands of bird-voices." Flocks of auks flitted above his head. He gazed at the dark cliffs up the coast and at the glaciers and icy plains "unseen by any human eye."

Suddenly he heard what sounded like a dog barking.

But how could that be? He listened again to the wind, but this time heard only the "bubbling noise of thousands of birds."

I must have been mistaken, he thought, but again he heard a barking sound—"first single barks, then full cry; there was one deep bark, and one sharper." *Yes,* he thought, *it sounds like barking dogs,* but was it?

At that moment, he recalled hearing two loud bangs like gun-shots the day before. He had figured it was just the cracking ice. Now he was not so sure.

Nansen shouted to Johansen, "I heard dogs barking," and his companion tumbled out of the tent.

"Dogs?" He rubbed the sleep from his eyes. Then Johansen put his ears to the wind to listen.

After a while, he said yes, maybe it could be dogs, or thousands of birds hatching in the nearby rocks.

Nansen decided to investigate. He gobbled his food, grabbed skis, telescope, gun, and cartridges, and left Johansen to guard the kayaks.

The last camp.

Nansen set off in doubt, but only a few hundred yards from camp, he found animal tracks much too large to be fox. Distinctly canine. Wolf tracks? Again he heard a dog yelping.

Now he felt really strange walking over the hummocks, and his pace quickened.

Suddenly he heard a shout. A human voice. The blood rushed to his brain. His heart pounded.

He scrambled up another hummock and hollered, "Halloo," with all he had in his lungs. And then he was racing on the ice ridges as fast as his legs could carry him.

A dark form moved toward him over the ice. It *was* a dog. And farther off was another figure—a man.

Who?

The two men hurried toward each other. Nansen waved his hat; the other man waved his hat, too.

Nansen heard the man speak English to the dogs, and he instantly recognized Frederick George Jackson, the British polar explorer. Jackson was well groomed and wore an English check suit and high rubber boots.

The two men shook hands. Jackson smelled of scented soap.

On June 17, 1896, Nansen had his first encounter with a stranger: Frederick George Jackson, British officer and researcher. This photo was re-created six days after the meeting.

But could this really be the explorer who had planned to explore Franz Josef Land just after Nansen and the *Fram* had left Kristiania?

At first, Jackson had no idea who Nansen was. All he saw was "a tall man, wearing a soft felt hat, loosely made, voluminous clothes and long shaggy hair and beard, all reeking with black grease."

"So glad to see you," said Jackson. "Have you a ship here? . . . How many are there of you?"

"One companion at the ice-edge."

They talked as they walked, and Jackson kept thinking this fellow must be shipwrecked.

Suddenly Jackson stopped, turned, and fixed his eyes on Nansen's face. "Aren't you Nansen?"

"Yes, I am."

"By Jove! I am glad to see you!" Jackson again seized Nansen's hand and shook it really hard this time, his whole face and dark eyes beaming. Jackson had been an early applicant to go with Nansen on the *Fram*.

As they walked, Nansen recounted the tale of his attempt to reach the North Pole.

Again Jackson shook the Norwegian's hand.

"So glad to be the first person to congratulate you on your return." He could not stop smiling. Jackson said, "I have plenty of room for you and expect my ship any day."

They fired shots in the air to let Johansen know all was well, and when six of Jackson's crew greeted Nansen on the ice, a triple British cheer "from seven power lungs" echoed among the hummocks.

Some of the men immediately went to fetch Johansen and carry the boats and sleds back to Jackson's base camp.

GETTING JOHANSEN

⟶

*A*S SOON AS Nansen had left camp to investigate the dog sounds, Johansen scurried up the hummock and put his ears to the wind. First, he heard birds. Then he heard the distinct sound of dogs barking. *Who could it be?* he wondered. He scurried back to camp and waited excitedly for Nansen to return with news. He never heard any gunshots; perhaps the wind had taken the sound in a different direction.

One of Johansen's dark shirts was flying high on a pole on the hummock above their camp to signal where Nansen should return. Coming toward him now was a dark figure against the blinding white and uneven ice. But the man approaching was not on skis. One of Jackson's men was walking with a gun over his shoulder, his legs awkward from sinking into the snow.

Johansen quickly ran a Norwegian flag up the pole, so the stranger would know he was Norwegian.

The man waved his hat. Waving his own greasy cap, Johansen ran toward him. They shook hands. Johansen could smell the soap on the clean-shaven man, who asked, "English?"

"No," Johansen answered and was immediately frustrated because he did not speak English. He tried German and French, but neither spoke the other's languages. They resorted to the universal language of pointing and pantomime.

When others from Jackson's expedition arrived, they took off their hats and gave hearty cheers to the Norwegian flag. Johansen was overcome with many feelings standing there like a wild man in rags, surrounded by the ice that he and Nansen had struggled against for three years. Above waved the little Norwegian flag, which made Johansen feel so proud of his country as the Englishmen's cheers rang out across the bleak fields of ice.

Everyone helped Johansen break up camp. Happily he threw away the leftover blubber and bear's flesh. The Englishmen would not let Johansen carry anything back to Jackson's base camp. One man put a pipe into his mouth; someone gave him tobacco; then they set off, three to a sled.

It was like a dream. Johansen, carefree on only one ski, like a skateboard, smoking his pipe like a sea captain, spotted the Englishmen's houses ahead, just above the shore. He saw Nansen, with his long hair and blackened face, standing outside the big house, posing for a photograph. Johansen waved his hat at Nansen, who waved back.

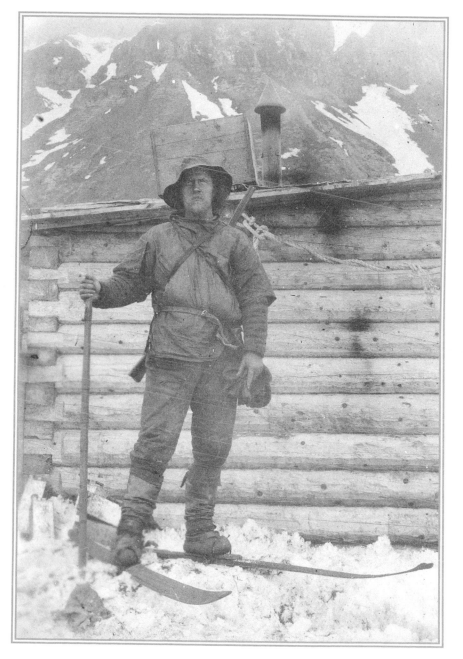

Nansen outside Jackson's cabin.

Johansen outside Jackson's cabin.

JACKSON'S HOUSE

BUILT ON A flat terrace beneath a mountain, only fifty feet from the sea, Jackson's winter quarters consisted of a main dwelling, a log cabin he called Elmwood, along with four octagonal wood-and-canvas storage huts, a doghouse, and a stable for ponies. He and his men had been here at Cape Flora off and on for almost two years, making this a semipermanent staging ground for the exploration of the archipelago of Franz Josef Land. Amazingly, this was the very place on Northbrook Island where Leigh Smith's crew of twenty-five men had built their hut after the steamer *Eira* got nipped and crushed by ice in 1881.

This photo shows Jackson's meteorological station in Elmwood. From left to right: a Russian log cabin, a stable for horses, and four round equipment tents.

Nansen felt odd entering Jackson's house, this "comfortable, warm nest in the midst of these desolate, wintry surroundings." Photographs and etchings covered the walls, along with shelves of books and all kinds of scientific and navigational instruments. A coal-fired stove was drying clothes and boots.

Nansen sat down in a comfortable chair with a strange feeling in his gut. Everything felt so different now. In one single instant, three long years of troubles were swept away. How could it be that only a few days ago, a walrus had attacked him, and before that, he had been swimming for both of their lives to save the kayaks?

Now he was surrounded by all the luxuries he and Johansen had dreamed about for months. The journey was over. All he had to do was wait a few weeks for Jackson's supply sloop to return from London to carry him and Johansen back home.

Frederick George Jackson in front of his meteorological station.

Jackson passed Nansen a packet of letters from Norway (he'd brought letters for Nansen and a few other crew members in case the two expeditions should meet, but there was no letter for Johansen). Nansen's heart beat hard as he carefully read them. Though two years old, his letters from home contained only good tidings. Eva and Liv were well.

A deep feeling of peace settled upon Nansen's soul.

Part Thirteen

NORWAY

JUNE 18–AUGUST 12, 1896

Freshly groomed Johansen with a book in Jackson's cabin.

VANISHING CAVEMEN

———————————————————→

LOOKING AT HIMSELF in a mirror, Johansen hardly recognized the creature staring back. The greatest comfort for him and Nansen was throwing off their dirty rags, bathing in warm water, and scrubbing the grime out of their skin. The cleaning process took days. They cut their hair and shaved their beards and put on soft, clean clothes. They loved moving around without their old rags sticking to their bodies. They ate bread, butter, milk, sugar, and coffee. They had dinner with real forks and knives, and the "transformation from savage to European was complete."

Nansen looked over at Johansen, his "comrade of the long winter night," and searched "in vain for any trace of the tramp who wandered up and down that desolate shore" beneath the cliff, outside their half-submerged winter hut. The caveman had vanished. Now he saw a "healthy-looking European citizen in a comfortable chair, puffing away at a short pipe . . . with a book before him, doing his best to learn English." Nansen helped his friend in his studies of English by agreeing to speak to him only in English.

TIME WITH JACKSON

July 10

*I*T WAS JUST over three years since Nansen had left his house in Kristiania and walked down through the gardens in the rain to the little launch of the *Fram*, then looked up to see his daughter laughing and clapping her hands. Nansen was eager to get home, but Jackson's ship, the *Windward*, was delayed. Jackson assured him it would arrive any day.

Nansen could hardly believe what good fortune it was that he and his companion had fallen into the hands of such kind and welcoming people. He and Jackson had so much in common. They never tired of talking. It was as if they'd known each other not for days, but for years. Like Nansen, Jackson was an expedition leader recording new information about the Arctic. He collected Arctic specimens and discovered and mapped new islands. He was a similarly educated man.

Nansen discovered their watches were indeed off by almost twenty-six minutes, making it necessary to alter his recorded readings of longitude by 6.5°, or about forty-one miles. He ran through his notebooks making corrections. He planned to make more accurate calculations when he returned to Norway.

With lots of time on his hands, Nansen explored Cape Flora with Jackson. They collected fossils and recorded scientific observations on the geology of the region. They took long hikes and shot birds. Nansen began to sketch a new map of Franz Josef Land, comparing his own geographical discoveries with the maps of Jackson, Payer, and Leigh Smith.

Nansen on skis.

He discussed with Jackson what to call the unnamed lands they had explored in the archipelago. Out of gratitude to the Englishman, Nansen named the island where he and Johansen had spent the winter Frederick Jackson's Island.

THE *WINDWARD*

←——————————————————————————

July 20

*T*HE *WINDWARD* **WAS** long overdue. Nansen and Johansen began to fear Jackson's ship had gotten stuck in ice and they might be forced to remain with the Englishmen all winter. The wind had already started to bring massive ice floes toward land. Some days when they looked out to sea, their hearts dropped to notice an interminable frozen white expanse. They wondered aloud if they should just paddle across the sea as planned, to Spitsbergen, to that "Tromsø sloop" that they'd dreamed about for so long.

They decided it was better to stay and wait.

Nearly a week later, Jackson tugged on Nansen's leg to wake him up.

"The ship is here! The ship is here!" The Englishman was beaming.

Nansen jumped out of bed and ran to the window, and there she was "just beyond the edge of the ice, steaming slowly in to find an anchorage. Wonderful to see a ship again! How high the rigging seemed, and the hull! It was like an island. There would be tidings on board from the great world far beyond."

When Nansen went aboard, the crew of the *Windward* raised a hearty British cheer for Nansen's return from the ice. Captain Brown said the whole world had suddenly become interested in Arctic regions as never before, that Spitsbergen had swelled with tourists arriving on steamers, that the Swedish explorer Salomon August

Andrée was poised and waiting for the right wind to take his balloon from Spitsbergen to the North Pole.

Days passed before the *Windward* could depart, and the ice was a growing problem. When the small boat finally ferried Nansen and Johansen to the ship, two colliding ice floes nearly crushed the launch. The men rowed as hard as they could and got to the ship moments before the floes crashed and crumbled into each other. It was as if the Arctic was trying to prevent the two survivors from leaving its frozen grip.

At last, the *Windward* set sail, deftly dodging ice floes. The captain sat in the crow's nest for days on end, skillfully guiding the boat through so much gathering ice. On August 11, it broke free into open water. Nansen and Johansen finally left the pack ice that had held them captive for three long years.

RETURN TO VARDØ

August 12

F ROM THE DECK of the *Windward*, Nansen spied something dark and low on the horizon. He peered into the evening light again, until a bare and naked coast came slowly into view—it was the shoreline of his beloved Norway.

Few, if anyone, spotted the *Windward* early the next morning gliding into the peaceful harbor at Vardø. Nansen and Johansen jumped into a skiff and headed immediately for the telegraph station in town.

Ashore, they stamped their feet on the ground to feel their native soil. A few people walking by them stared at Johansen's odd jacket that he'd made from a blanket back in their winter hut. A cow in the street gazed at them. Nansen wanted to pet the cow because it looked so "summery."

The S.Y. Windward, *photographed in Queens Wharf before the beginning of Jackson's Arctic expedition.*

Part Fourteen

HOME

AUGUST 13—SEPTEMBER 9, 1896

VARDØ

→

*A*T THE TELEGRAPH office, Nansen learned that his friend and mentor Henrik Mohn just happened to be in town, the very man whose writings had given him the idea for the *Fram* Expedition. Nansen immediately went to the hotel to seek him out. How strange it seemed that the first friend he would meet back home would be this fellow.

News of Nansen's arrival in Vardø drew crowds. Everyone wanted "to see the two polar bears who strode through the streets to the hotel."

Nansen shoved Mohn's hotel room door open, and there "lay Mohn on the sofa, reading, with a long pipe in his mouth. He started up and stared fixedly, like a madman, at the long figure standing on the threshold; his pipe fell to the ground, his face twitched, and then he burst out, 'Can it be true? Is it Fridtjof Nansen?'"

When he heard Nansen's voice, he knew this was no ghost. He cried out, "Thank God, you're still alive!" and rushed over to hug his friend, and then he hugged Johansen.

Everyone talked at once and asked one another a million questions and gave a million answers. Then Nansen sat down and more soberly related what had happened during his three-year absence.

They drank champagne and smoked cigars while the street outside swarmed with smiling townsfolk. The Norwegian flag was raised in the evening sunshine on the masts of every boat in the harbor. A band played Norway's national anthem outside the hotel windows. "And then came telegrams in torrents, all of them bringing good news."

Their troubles were over. *Yet,* Nansen thought, *the joy is not complete until there is good news from the* Fram.

EVA AND LIV

Kristiania, Norway

August 13

THAT SAME DAY, back in Kristiania, around seven in the evening, one of Nansen's neighbors reported, "My wife and I were walking along the private path leading to our own and the Nansens' houses, and which belongs to them and us together. Little four-year-old Liv Nansen met us and chattered, 'Mamma has gone to town. Papa is coming home.'"

A telegram from Nansen had arrived that read "Home safe after fortunate expedition." Eva had immediately set out for the center of town to tell her mother, and to hear more news.

Masses of people began to swarm the streets of Kristiania. The cafés were full. Every new telegram that came into a newspaper office was posted outside, where crowds pushed and shoved to read them. Groups of people shouted and sang national songs. A parade of fishing vessels gathered in front of Nansen's house on the fjord. The fishermen took off their hats and shouted "Hurrah!" over and over.

Eva planned an immediate journey up the coast of Norway to meet her husband. A visiting neighbor said to her, "What a wonderful thing it is for you, after three anxious years!"

Eva replied with a smile, "I never doubted he would return."

Hammerfest today.

August 16

Three days later, Nansen and Johansen sailed into the harbor at Hammerfest, where the whole town greeted them on the docks. Eva was waiting jubilantly to join her husband.

The yacht Otaria *at Hammerfest, where Nansen was greeted by Sir George Baden-Powel.*

August 20

A telegram arrived in Hammerfest. With Johansen at his side, Nansen tore it open and read:

Fridtjof Nansen:
Fram arrived in good condition. All well on board. Shall start at once for Tromsø. Welcome home!

Otto Sverdrup

The *Fram* had broken out of the pack ice and reached safety! Nansen stared at the words. He felt like choking. All he could say was "The *Fram* has arrived!" Johansen's face radiated happiness. Nansen raced to tell Eva the ship was safe. News quickly spread around town. People rushed through the streets, wild with joy.

It felt just like the ending of a fairy tale. Nansen read and reread the telegram until he felt a happiness he'd never experienced before.

Nansen, Eva, and Johansen set out at once for Tromsø.

The Fram *anchored in Tromsø.*

TROMSØ REUNION

August 21

*I*N TROMSØ HARBOR, the *Fram*, which Nansen had last seen buried in towers of ice, though now a little battered and weather-beaten, floated free and proud, still strong and stalwart, on the deep blue sea. The merry waves lapped at her steadfast hull.

Nansen and his group cried out, "Three cheers for the *Fram!*" to which the crew returned, "Hurrah!" as they jumped into a boat and rowed over to Nansen, most of them still dressed in their Arctic clothes, some with long beards. Bentsen was in the bow, and Scott-Hansen in the middle of the boat. Here, too, was Peder Hendriksen, who had been the last to watch Nansen and Johansen with their sleds and dogs heading northward into the unknown fifteen months ago.

Everyone waved, beaming with joy. Johansen leaned over the railing and shouted, "Welcome, boys!" Bentsen grabbed Johansen's hand and tried to pull him down into the boat. Everyone now jumped over the railing, and Nansen said, "You have done well," but nobody was thinking clearly. Nothing mattered except that they had "escaped unscathed the terrors of the ice-desert" and were all together again in Norway. The expedition had completed its task.

WHAT HAD HAPPENED TO THE *FRAM*?

March 14, 1895–August 21, 1896

AFTER NANSEN AND Johansen had left the ship, the *Fram* continued to drift in ice for another seventeen months. As commander of the eleven remaining crew on board, Sverdrup continued to collect scientific data, observations of ice, sea depth, sea temperatures, and sea chemistry that Nansen wanted.

Then on August 13, 1896, one day after Nansen arrived in Vardø, the *Fram* shook off the last of the ice floes.

The Fram *moving in ice.*

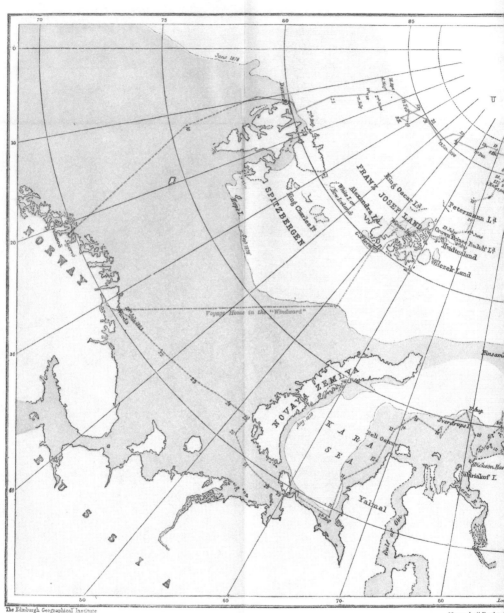

The Edinburgh Geographical Institute

Nansen's " Farthest

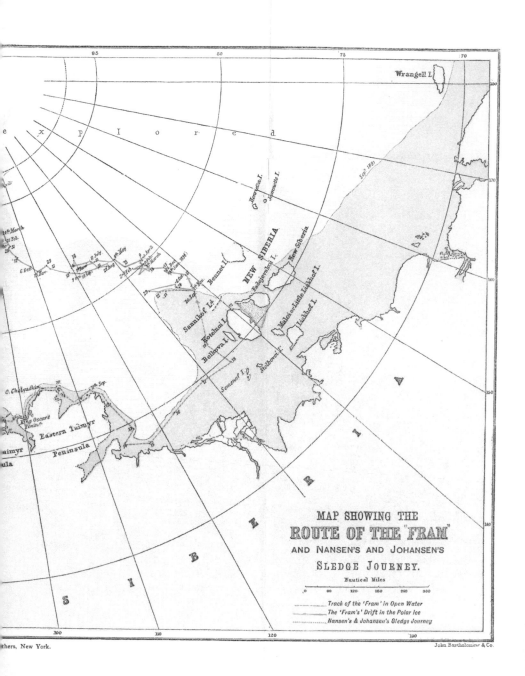

MAP SHOWING THE
ROUTE OF THE "FRAM"
AND NANSEN'S AND JOHANSEN'S
SLEDGE JOURNEY.

Nautical Miles

0   60   120   180   240   300

———————— Track of the 'Fram' in Open Water
—————————— The 'Fram's' Drift in the Polar Ice
··············· Nansen's & Johansen's Sledge Journey

thers, New York.

John Bartholomew & Co.

They were free! Mixed feelings overcame the crew. It was hard to believe they were plowing through deep ocean water and headed directly to the northern coast of the big island of Spitsbergen. As in a dream, the water lapped at the ship, which "gently pitched with the first feeble swells."

The ship at the edge of the ice.

The men fired a salute from the ship's cannons as they watched the disappearing outline of the ice floes, with those frozen ridges and hummocks. A great mist descended on the ice as it disappeared behind them forever.

They sailed southeast in a dense fog. A Norwegian whaling ship came alongside but had no news of Nansen. When they reached Danes Island, the crew saw land for the first time in 1,041 days. The explorer Andrée, who was there waiting for winds to carry his balloon to the North Pole, came out to greet them. He, too, had no news of Nansen.

Finally, on August 20, just eight days after Nansen and Johansen reached Vardø, the *Fram* itself steamed into a little harbor on the Norwegian mainland.

At the small telegraph office, Sverdrup discovered that Nansen had returned from the ice only days before. Overjoyed, he ran back to the ship, and the *Fram* gave a cannon salute. Incredibly relieved that their friends were still alive, the crew could begin to appreciate the paradise of flowers and grass and trees all about them, sights they had not seen in years.

Full-steam, the *Fram* headed for Tromsø and the reunion.

Fridtjof and Eva Nansen on the Otaria.

KRISTIANIA

*A*FTER DAYS OF celebration in Tromsø, the *Fram* set sail for Kristiania, with its full original crew aboard, still more than a thousand miles away. In every port, from "steamers crowded with holiday-making townsfolk, and from the poorest fishing-boat," the hearts of all Norwegians went out to them. They were hugged and thanked for all they had done.

Johansen thought it a "splendid reward for all our hardships," and felt deeply satisfied to make Norway proud. Nansen wondered what they had really accomplished except their duty. He knew they owed Norway their gratitude.

Steamboats loaded with people swarmed around the *Fram* in the Kristiania harbor. Thousands waited for them on shore. Flags flew everywhere. Handkerchiefs and hats waved in the air, and the fjord bulged with a multitude of radiant faces.

Nansen could see his home, with the little beach below shining in the sunlight. "Then steamers on steamers again, shouts after shouts; and we all stood, hat in hand, bowing as they cheered."

The Fram *after returning to Kristiania.*

Later that evening when the echoes of celebration had died away, Nansen walked alone down to the beach in front of his house. The spruce woods stood silent all around him. The embers of a bonfire smoldered on a nearby headland. The sea rippled at his feet and seemed to whisper, *Now you are home.*

The deep peace of the autumn evening drew over his weary spirit as he recalled that rainy June morning when he had hopped into the launch and set off in the gloom of an uncertain future. "More than three years had passed; we had toiled and we had sown, and now the harvest had come. In my heart I sobbed and wept for joy and thankfulness."

All that interminable ice and those endless moonlit polar nights were like far-off dreams from another world, dreams he had had long ago that were now passing away like mist.

Yet, he thought, *What would life be worth without its dreams?*

Fridtjof Nansen with daughter Liv in his arms.

Epilogue

1896-1930

NANSEN'S EXPEDITION IN the frozen *Fram*, floating and drifting on the pack ice, then his daring dash with Johansen across the Arctic wasteland by sled and kayak, contributed the largest single advance in Arctic knowledge in nearly four hundred years of polar exploration.

Ink-and-pen watercolor by Nansen of a polar landscape.

Fridtjof Nansen's first portrait in Norway after the expedition.

Before Nansen made his run for the pole, he and Sverdrup had talked about making a future attempt at the South Pole with the *Fram*. Nansen had wanted to be the first man ever to reach both South and North Poles, but when he finally returned home, Nansen chose to give up polar exploration to pursue other lofty goals.

Future polar explorers would come to talk to Nansen before they set out on their own journeys. Americans Dr. Frederick A. Cook, Rear Admiral Robert E. Peary, and Matthew Henson claimed to reach the North Pole in 1908 and 1909. Sir Ernest Shackleton set off for the South Pole but missed the mark by 97 nautical miles, while fellow Norwegian Roald Amundsen succeeded in reaching it in 1911, a matter of weeks before Robert Falcon Scott arrived. Amundsen used Nansen's *Fram* and called his base camp on the Bay of Whales "Framheim."

Nansen poses for a photo with his family.
In front, from left to right: *Irmelin, Eva Nansen with Odd in her arms, Kåre, and Liv.*

Nansen had approached polar travel with a scientist's attention to precision and detail. He had learned from the mistakes of previous Arctic explorers and emphasized the need for proper clothing and nutrition on long, hard journeys. He invented new ways to make polar travel successful and was one of the first to value the ways of traditional Inuit travel in the north. He tested every type of food and invented nutritious, though odd-sounding, foods like meat-chocolate.

Most of all, Nansen had boundless confidence and curiosity. Indeed, he did take chances, but they were well thought out and planned. *Fram* was the perfect name for his life, as well as his ship. He had great confidence in moving forward, and he blended physical strength with intelligence. While battling the Arctic at −40°C, he was single-minded and tenacious.

The remarkably solid vessel Colin Archer had built to "float" on the ice and carry Nansen to the pole was later used by Otto Sverdrup, from 1898 to 1902, to explore the Canadian Arctic, then by Roald Amundsen, from 1910 to 1912, when Amundsen succeeded in reaching the South Pole. The *Fram* now sits proudly in its own museum in Oslo.

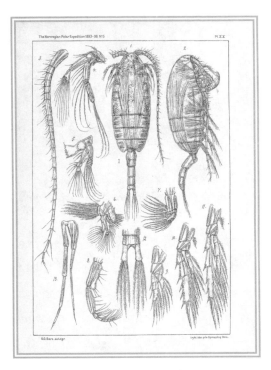

Drawings taken from Nansen's scientific report.

In 1897 Nansen took a position in zoology at the university in Kristiania and became a full professor of oceanography in 1908. His *Fram* Expedition led to more than six volumes of scientific data and findings, valuable information on the bottom deposits of the Arctic Ocean, the natural history of Arctic birds and small marine animals, the astronomy and climate of the Arctic, and so much more. His observations on board the *Fram* put an end to the fantasies of land, or an open sea, beyond the Arctic ice. No longer would people think of the Arctic Ocean as a shallow sea, either. Nansen measured the underwater depths of the seafloor and came up with readings greater than twelve thousand feet, or over two miles. Once and for all, Nansen's three-year trip helped define the Arctic as a solid cap of polar ice.

The net that Fridtjof Nansen constructed for the collection of plankton.

Later, he continued his oceanographic work in other parts of the Arctic, and many of his observations inspired other scientists to develop important physical processes in oceanography.

Portrait of Nansen during a stay in the United States.

Although Nansen gave up polar exploration, he went on to an illustrious career as a statesman and diplomat, serving the newly formed kingdom of Norway after it separated from Sweden in 1905. He helped found the League of Nations, the forerunner of the United Nations, and he worked with displaced prisoners after World War I, which had left two to three million ex-prisoners dispersed throughout Russia. Nansen helped resettle Armenian refugees from Turkey and provide famine relief in central Russia and the Ukraine. Led by Fridtjof Nansen, the Commission for Refugees also established the Nansen Passport as a means of identifying stateless people.

Fridtjof Nansen visited an orphanage during a trip to Armenia,
where he was sponsored by the International Labour Union and the League of Nations,
in order to examine refugee relief opportunities in the summer of 1925.

The Nansen Passport was issued to Russians and other refugees who were not given access
to ordinary passports, and was honored by the governments of fifty-two nations.

For his humanitarian work in international diplomacy, Nansen was awarded the Nobel Peace Prize in 1922. A driven man with a great and restless spirit, he is remembered as much today for the compassion he showed for millions of starving and displaced people as he is for his Arctic successes.

Nansen and the Norwegian Arctic expedition on the Fram
after their homecoming in Kristiania.

The crew of the *Fram* returned home to Norway as heroes, and, like many of the men, Johansen continued to explore the Arctic. On Nansen's recommendation, he accompanied Roald Amundsen aboard the *Fram* in 1910 to Antarctica. Near the South Pole, Johansen rescued a less experienced member of the expedition in a blizzard in windchills of −50°C (−58°F), but because of a disagreement with Amundsen, he was not allowed to accompany the main group on the world's first successful trip to the South Pole. In fact, Amundsen never credited Johansen with his heroic deed or even with being part of the South Pole expedition; there had been such bad blood between them. Johansen never recovered from the humiliation of Amundsen's anger. He took to drink and committed suicide in 1913.

Johansen in front of the Fram, *which is locked in ice.*

In an obituary for Johansen, Nansen described his companion as a brave man, a trustworthy and faithful friend, "so straightforward and simple, so quiet and taciturn, a soul that knew no betrayal." He recalled Johansen's cool under pressure:

When he was struck down by a bear, he lay calmly underneath it, grabbing it by the throat while he waited for me, who was fumbling with the kayak to get hold of the rifle; he said nothing until the bear bared its teeth to grab his skull, then it came: "Look sharp, or it'll be too late." But the instant the bear turned against the dogs, Johansen got on his feet again and dived for his rifle, when at last the shot ran out and the bear fell.

Fridtjof Nansen with his children after Eva's death.
From the left: *Liv, Odd, Åsmund,* and *Kåre. Nansen is holding Irmelin in his arms.*

Nansen forged on through his own personal loss. He and Eva had two daughters and three sons, but Eva died of pneumonia in 1907, and their youngest son, Åsmund, died after a long illness in 1913. Throughout all this, Nansen never gave up science or the chance for the next expedition. He even planned a trip to the North Pole in a zeppelin, a giant airship inflated with gas.

This drawing depicts the airship Graf Zeppelin above the Arctic Sea. Nansen had imagined that humans could measure depth without having to land on ice through the use of sonar.

Fridtjof Nansen at his desk.

On May 13, 1930, Nansen died at the age of sixty-eight of a heart attack at his home, sitting on the veranda drinking tea and working on a scientific manuscript. He was buried on Norway's National Day, May 17, the same holiday he had celebrated on board the *Fram* with his crew and then again with Johansen in their cold stone hut on that uncharted island in Franz Josef Land.

The nation of Norway honored one of their greatest heroes by packing the streets of Oslo (the name was changed from Kristiania in 1924) with thousands who wanted to pay their last respects. A procession of schoolchildren marched through the city to the university, where Nansen's coffin was covered with a Norwegian flag. The bands stopped playing; the singing choirs fell silent. The Norwegian royal family offered flowers. Nearby stood the secretariat of the League of Nations and representatives from almost every government in the world.

Nansen's burial procession on May 17, 1930.

Nansen's Arctic companion from both the Greenland and *Fram* journeys, Otto Sverdrup, stood near his coffin.

Flags throughout the city were lowered to half-mast. A cannon gave the signal for a two-minute silence throughout the country. And Fridtjof Nansen was laid to rest.

Nansen's gravesite.

When the *Fram* had left Norway thirty-seven years before and seemed to disappear off the face of the planet, only to return three years later with Nansen and his crew alive and well, Nansen became a hero throughout the world. He had revolutionized polar travel with dogs, sleds, kayaks, and skis. Against all advice, he had locked his tiny wooden ship into the frozen Arctic Sea and slowly floated north toward the pole. Then he and Johansen had skied seven hundred miles, surviving fifteen months on the pack ice.

Fridtjof Nansen, scientist, humanitarian, and Renaissance man was one of the greatest polar explorers of all time.

Portrait of Fridtjof Nansen's as the League of Nations'
high commissioner for prisoners of war and refugees.

Author's Note

*T*HE STORY OF Fridtjof Nansen's 1893–96 Arctic journey ranks right up there with Ernest Shackleton's epic polar adventure among the most incredible adventure tales of all time. There are nearly fifty books about Ernest Shackleton, yet Nansen's underreported story comes from only three books: (1) his own account, *Farthest North: The Epic Adventure of a Visionary Explorer*, which *National Geographic* called "One of the 100 greatest adventure books of all time"; (2) Hjalmar Johansen's account of his survival tale, *With Nansen in the North: A Record of the* Fram *Expedition in 1893–96*; and (3) Roland Huntford's excellent biography of Nansen called *Nansen: The Explorer as Hero*. Nansen's tale shows up as a chapter in various adventure compendiums, but it surely warrants more book treatment, as I attempt here. Twenty years before Shackleton's famous *Endurance* tale, Nansen was the first to bring everyone home alive.

I have drawn on these three books and on other accounts of polar explorers who traipsed through that wonderfully cold and bleak region. I have also been to the Arctic many times. One essential resource for me has been my friend Geoff Carroll from Barrow, Alaska. In 1986, after fifty-five days of mushing from March to May, Geoff and five others reached the North Pole. Just as Nansen and Johansen did, Geoff kept a journal that captures a sense of the place and the struggle it takes to embark on such an adventure. No question that the ice has changed since Nansen's day. No longer does it freeze up in August and September the way it did for Nansen above Siberia. Things are changing so fast in the Arctic that even Geoff's polar experience in 1986 probably could not be repeated today.

HUNTING ANIMALS
AND USING SLED DOGS FOR POLAR TRAVEL

Hunting animals in the age of polar exploration was a necessity. Everything the men killed was used for food or clothing and other essentials. Attitudes toward the dogs, too, were very different in those days. Sled dogs were working animals, rather than simply pets. Although they might be given names by men who cared for them, they often had more in common with their wolf ancestors than with domesticated dogs. In the early days of polar exploration, dogs were often eaten, if not by other dogs in order to sustain them, then by the men trying to survive out on the ice. On his first attempt to reach the North Pole in 1906, bad weather beset American polar explorer Admiral Robert E. Peary. His stronger, more useful dogs survived off the flesh of their companions. Then, finally, the men sacrificed all the remaining dogs except one for consumption to survive. On Roald Amundsen's successful South Pole journey in 1911, the expedition set off with fifty-two dogs, returning with only eleven. Most had been killed at stages along the way and were eaten by men and dogs alike.

WHAT AND WHERE IS THE NORTH POLE?

The North Pole is the northernmost place on Earth and is located in the Arctic Ocean, which is covered by a large sheet of floating ice that is in constant motion. There is no land at the North Pole. To pinpoint it on the globe, imagine that the planet rotates around an imaginary vertical line, or axis, running through the center of the earth like a big nail. The nail would exit in two places, the North Pole at the top, and the South Pole at the bottom.

From the North Pole, any direction you face is south. The nearest land is about seven hundred miles away. Although the North Pole is an actual place, the ice is ever-shifting, so it is difficult to locate it without navigational instruments, either with the more traditional sextant or modern GPS (Global Positioning System) devices. Today the pole is reached by icebreaker ship, plane, or surface travel (dogsled, snow machine, and on foot).

During the summer, the sun never sets at the North Pole. It rises in March and finally sets in September. Conversely, in the winter months, the sun never rises. Polar bears live in the Arctic near the North Pole. Penguins live at the South Pole.

On the subject of distances from the pole, I have found discrepancies in various narratives. Amazingly, there seem to be disagreements on specific locations that explorers reached and how close to the pole they got. Checking multiple sources, I've done my best in each case to determine accurate figures.

I hope readers get a feel for polar travel and what it was like for explorers before the age of cell and satellite phones and other hand-held digital devices that now can take pinpoint readings. To navigate on the ice, Nansen relied on taking readings of the sun and other celestial bodies with the sextant and theodolite, as well as simple watches and compasses.

Homeward after sunset.

After

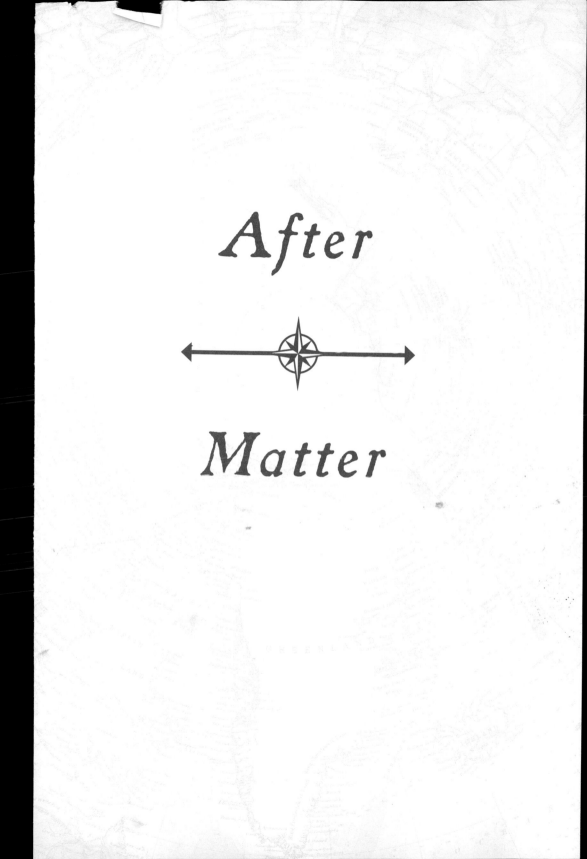

Matter

Second lieutenant Sigurd Scott-Hansen,
who was responsible for the meteorological, astronomical, and magnetic observations
on the expedition, turned out to be a good photographer.

Appendix

- THE DESIGN OF THE *FRAM*
- THE CREW OF THE *FRAM*
- DUTIES OF THE CREW ABOARD
- SCIENCE ABOARD THE *FRAM*
- FULL LIST OF NANSEN'S EQUIPMENT FOR THE TWO-MAN DASH
  TO THE NORTH POLE
- A LIST OF NANSEN'S DOGS ON STARTING THE TREK
  TO THE NORTH POLE
- DOGS AND POLAR EXPLORATION
- NORTH POLE EXPEDITIONS AND RECORDS OF FARTHEST NORTH
- A SPECIAL NOTE ON GEOFF CARROLL AND A MODERN-DAY SLED DOG
  TRIP TO THE NORTH POLE
- NAVIGATING IN THE ARCTIC
  - EXPLANATION OF NAVIGATING AT THE NORTH POLE, BY PAUL SCHURKE
  - SIMPLE USE OF THE SUN AND A 24-HOUR WATCH, BY GEOFF CARROLL
- TIME LINE
- GLOSSARY

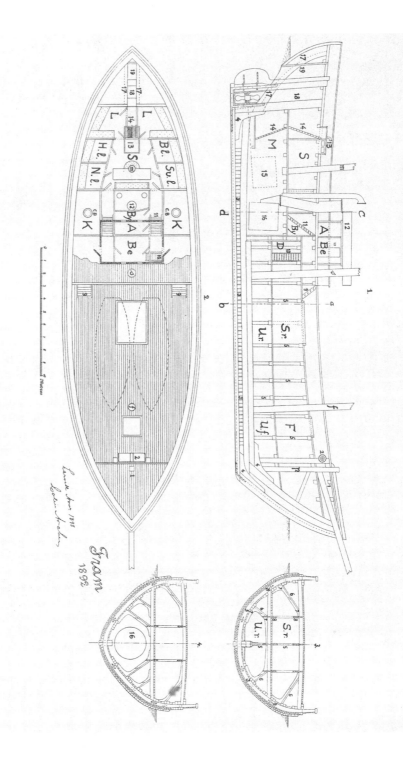

Fram
1892

The Design of the Fram

NANSEN OBSERVED THAT many Arctic explorers never really gave much thought to their boats but took what was available. He felt that the success of the *Fram* Expedition depended on having the right ship built for the ice. For living quarters, a series of small cabins opened up to the saloon, where eating and social activity took place. The *Fram* had four single cabins, one each for Nansen, Sverdrup, Scott-Hansen, and Dr. Blessing. Two larger cabins housed either four men or five: Amundsen, Pettersen, Juell, and Johansen shared one, and Mogstad, Bentsen, Jacobsen, Nordahl, and Hendriksen were cramped together.

Printed replica of Archer's construction drawings for the Fram.

The Crew of the Fram

*H*UNDREDS OF APPLICANTS from all over the world wanted to join Nansen's North Pole journey. Each man had to be in peak condition. Nansen wrote in *Farthest North* about his final choices in crew:

> And here on board are men who are leaving wife and children behind them. How sad has been the separation! what longing, what yearning, await them in the coming years! And it is not for profit they do it. For honor and glory then? These may be scant enough. It is the same thirst for achievement, the same craving to get beyond the limits of the known, which inspired this people in the Saga times that is stirring in them again to-day.

The following is a list of the members of the expedition as Nansen described them in *Farthest North* (1898, Vol. 1):

*Captain
Otto Sverdrup
with his pipe.*

OTTO NEUMANN SVERDRUP, commander of the *Fram*, was born in Bindal, in Helgeland, 1855. At the age of seventeen he went to sea, passed his mate's examination in 1878, and for some years was captain of a ship. In 1888–89 he took part in the Greenland expedition. As soon as he heard of the plan of the polar expedition he expressed his desire to accompany it, and I knew that I could not place the *Fram* in better hands. He is married, and has one child.

*Second lieutenant
Sigurd Scott-Hansen.*

SIGURD SCOTT-HANSEN, first lieutenant in the navy, undertook the management of the meteorological, astronomical, and magnetic observations. He was born in Christiania in 1868. After passing through the naval school at Horten, he became an officer in 1889, and first lieutenant in 1892. He is a son of Andreas Hansen, parish priest in Christiania.

*Doctor and botanist
Henrik Greve Blessing.*

HENRIK GREVE BLESSING, doctor and botanist to the expedition, was born in Drammen in 1866, where his father was at that time a clergyman. He became a student in 1885, and graduated in medicine in the spring of 1893.

*Ship's mate
Theodor Claudius
Jacobsen.*

THEODOR CLAUDIUS JACOBSEN, mate of the *Fram*, was born at Tromsø in 1855, where his father was a ship's captain, afterwards harbormaster and head pilot. At the age of fifteen he went to sea, and passed his mate's examination four years later. He spent two years in New Zealand, and from 1886–90 he went on voyages to the Arctic Sea as skipper of a Tromsø sloop. He is married, and has one child.

*Chief engineer
Anton Amundsen.*

ANTON AMUNDSEN, chief engineer of the *Fram*, was born at Horten in 1853. In 1884 he passed his technical examination, and soon afterwards his engineer's examination. For twenty-five years he has been in the navy, where he attained the rank of chief engineer. He is married, and has six children.

*Steward and cook
Adolf Juel.*

ADOLF JUELL, steward and cook of the *Fram*, was born in the parish of Skåtø, near Kragerø, in 1860. His father, Claus Nielsen, was a farmer and ship-owner. In 1879 he passed his mate's examination, and has been captain of a ship many years. He is married, and has four children.

*Second engineer
Lars Pettersen.*

LARS PETTERSEN, second engineer of the *Fram*, was born in 1860, at Borre, near Landskrona, in Sweden, of Norwegian parents. He is a fully qualified smith and machinist, in which capacity he has served in the Norwegian navy for several years. Is married, and has children.

*Lieutenant
Frederik Hjalmar
Johansen.*

FREDERIK HJALMAR JOHANSEN, lieutenant in the Reserve, was born at Skien in 1867, and matriculated at the University in 1886. In 1891–92 he went to the Military School and became a supernumerary officer. He was so eager to take part in the expedition that, as no other post could be found for him, he accepted that of stoker.

*Harpooner
Peder Leonard
Hendriksen.*

PEDER LEONARD HENDRIKSEN, harpooner, was born in Balsfjord, near Tromsø, in 1859. From childhood he has been a sailor, and from fourteen years old has gone on voyages to the Arctic Sea as harpooner and skipper. In 1888 he was shipwrecked off Novaya Zemlya in the sloop *Enigheden*, from Christiansund. He is married, and has four children.

Electrician, fireman, and meteorological assistant Bernhard Nordahl.

BERNHARD NORDAHL was born in Christiania in 1862. At the age of fourteen he entered the navy, and advanced to be a gunner. Subsequently he has done a little of everything, and, among other things, has worked as an electrical engineer. He had charge of the dynamo and electric installation on board, acted, moreover, as stoker, and for a time assisted in the meteorological observations. He is married, and has five children.

Ivar Otto Irgens Mogstad.

IVAR OTTO IRGENS MOGSTAD was born at Aure, in Nordmøre, in 1856. In 1877 passed his examination as first assistant, and from 1882 onward was one of the head keepers at the Gaustad Lunatic Asylum.

Sailor Bernt Bentsen.

BERNT BENTSEN, born in 1860, went to sea for several years. In 1890 he passed his mate's examination, since which he has sailed as mate in several voyages to the Arctic Sea. We engaged him at Tromsø, just as we were starting. It was 8.30 when he came on board to speak to me, and at 10 o'clock the *Fram* set sail.

Collecting fresh water on the ice near the ship.

Duties of the Crew Aboard

*T*HE MEN WERE never idle. The following passages from *Farthest North* illustrate just how busy the men were aboard the frozen *Fram*:

There was the care of the ship and rigging, the inspection of sails, ropes, etc., etc.; there were provisions of all kinds to be got out from the cases down in the hold, and handed over to the cook; there was ice—good, pure, fresh-water ice—to be found and carried to the galley to be melted for cooking, drinking, and washing water. Then, as already mentioned, there was always something doing in the various workshops. Now "Smith Lars" had to straighten the long-boat davits, which had been twisted by the waves in the Kara Sea; now it was a hook, a knife, a bear-trap, or something else to be forged. The tinsmith, again "Smith Lars," had to solder together a great tin pail for the ice-melting in the galley. The mechanician, Amundsen, would have an order for some instrument or other—perhaps a new current-gauge. The watchmaker, Mogstad, would have a thermograph to examine and clean, or a new spring to put into a watch. The sailmaker might have an order for a quantity of dog-harness. Then each man had to be his own shoemaker—make himself canvas boots with thick, warm, wooden soles, according to Sverdrup's newest pattern. Presently there would come an order to mechanician Amundsen for a supply of new zinc music-sheets for the organ— these being a brand-new invention of the leader of the expedition. The electrician would have to examine and clean the accumulator batteries, which were in danger of freezing. When at last the windmill was ready, it had to be attended to, turned according to the wind, etc. And when the wind was too strong some one had to climb up and reef the mill sails, which was not a pleasant occupation in this winter cold, and involved much breathing on fingers and rubbing of the tip of the nose. . . .

For the ship's doctor there was less occupation. He looked long and vainly for patients, and at last had to give it up and in despair take to doctoring the dogs. Once a month he too had to make his scientific observations, which consisted in the weighing of each man, and the counting of blood corpuscles, and estimating the amount of blood pigment, in order to ascertain the number of red-blood corpuscles and the quantity of red coloring matter (hæmoglobin) in the blood of each. This was also work that was watched with anxious interest, as every man thought he could tell from the result obtained how long it would be before scurvy overtook him.

Doctor Blessing collecting algae samples from both the salt and fresh water.

Science Aboard the Fram

*T*HE **OCEANOGRAPHIC INFORMATION** Nansen brought back continues to influence polar science today. The following passages come from Nansen's journal in *Farthest North*.

Johansen (left) assisting Scott-Hansen with scientific observations.

METEOROLOGY

The meteorological observations ... were taken every four hours day and night; indeed, for a considerable part of the time, every two hours. They kept one man, sometimes two, at work all day. It was Hansen who had the principal charge of this department, and his regular assistant until March, 1895, was Johansen, whose place was then taken by Nordahl.

Johansen, armed, guarding the magnetic observatory from polar bears.

POSITIONING

The night observations were taken by whoever was on watch. About every second day, when the weather was clear, Hansen and his assistant took the astronomical observation which ascertained our position. This was certainly the work which was followed with most interest by all the members of the expedition; and it was not uncommon to see Hansen's cabin, while he was making his calculations, besieged with idle spectators, waiting to hear the result—whether we had drifted north or south since the last observation, and how far. The state of feeling on board very much depended on these results.

MAGNETIC CONSTANT AND VARIOUS OBSERVATIONS

Hansen had also at stated periods to take observations to determine the magnetic constant in this unknown region. These were carried on at first in a tent, specially constructed for the purpose, which was soon erected on the ice; but later we built him a large snow hut, as being both more suitable and more comfortable.

Among our scientific pursuits may also be mentioned the determining of the temperature of the water and of its degree of saltness at varying depths; the collection and examination of such animals as are to be found in these northern seas; the ascertaining of the amount of electricity in the air; the observation of the formation of the ice, its growth and thickness, and of the temperature of the different layers of ice; the investigation of the currents in the water under it, etc., etc. I had the main charge of this department.

STUDY OF NORTHERN LIGHTS

There remains to be mentioned the regular observation of the aurora borealis, which we had a splendid opportunity of studying. After I had gone on with it for some time, Blessing undertook this part of my duties; and when I left the ship I made over to him all the other observations that were under my charge.

SOUNDINGS AND DREDGINGS

Not an inconsiderable item of our scientific work were the soundings and dredgings. At the greater depths it was such an undertaking that every one had to assist; and, from the way we were obliged to do it later, one sounding sometimes gave occupation for several days.

The meteorological observatory on ice.
From the left: *Sigurd Scott-Hansen and Bernhard Nordahl.*

NANSEN SAMPLING WATER ABOARD
THE *FRAM* IN 1894

Wednesday, October 17th. We are employed in taking deep-water temperatures. It is a doubtful pleasure at this time of year. Sometimes the water-lifter gets coated with ice, so that it will not close down below in the water, and has, therefore, to hang for ever so long each time; and sometimes it freezes tight during the observation after it is brought up, so that the water will not run out of it into the sample bottles, not to mention all the bother there is getting the apparatus ready to lower. We are lucky if we do not require to take the whole thing into the galley every time to thaw it. It is slow work; the temperatures have sometimes to be read by lantern light. The water samples are not so reliable, because they freeze in the lifter. But the thing can be done, and we must just go on doing it. The same easterly wind is blowing, and we are drifting onward. Our latitude this evening is about 81°47′ N.

Thursday, October 18th. I continue taking the temperatures of the water, rather a cool amusement with the thermometer down to -29°C. (20.2° Fahr. below zero) and a wind blowing. Your fingers are apt to get a little stiff and numb when you have to manipulate the wet or ice-covered metal screws with bare hands and have to read off the thermometer with a magnifying-glass in order to insure accuracy to the hundredth part of a degree, and then to bottle the samples of water, which you have to keep close against your breast, to prevent the water from freezing. It is a nice business!

Full List of Nansen's Equipment

for TWO-MAN DASH to the NORTH POLE

SLEDGE NO. 1 (WITH NANSEN'S KAYAK)	Lbs.	Oz.	Kilos.
Kayak	41	2	18.7
Pump (for pumping kayaks in case of leakage)	1	2	0.5
Sail	1	9	0.7
Axe and geological hammer	1	5	0.6
Gun and case	7	4	3.3
Two small wooden rods belonging to cooker	0	14	0.4
Theodolite and case	4	13	2.2
Three reserve cross-pieces for sledges	2	0	0.9
Some pieces of wood	0	11	0.3
Harpoon line	0	8.4	0.24
Fur gaiters	1	3	0.55
Five balls of cord	2	9	1.17
Cooker, with two mugs, ladle, and two spoons	8	13	4.0

Petroleum lamp (Primus)	0	4 1/2	0.1
Pocket-flask	0	6	0.17
Bag, with sundry articles of clothing	8	13	4.0
Blanket	4	6	2.0
Jersey	2	8	1.15
Finn shoes filled with grass	3	1	1.4
Cap for fitting over opening in kayak	0	7	0.2
One pair "komager"	2	1	0.95
Two pair kayak gloves and one harpoon and line	1	5	0.6
One waterproof sealskin kayak overcoat	3	1	1.4
Tool-bag	2	10	1.2
Bag of sewing materials, including sailmaker's palm, sail needles, and other sundries	2	10	1.2
Three Norwegian flags	0	4	0.1
Medicines, etc.	4	15	2.25
Photographic camera	4	10	2.1
One cassette and one tin box of films	3	14	1.75
One wooden cup	0	3	0.08
One rope (for lashing kayak to sledge)	2	0	0.9
Pieces of reindeer-skin to prevent kayaks from chafing	3	15	1.8
Wooden shovel	2	3	1.0
Ski-staff with disk at bottom	1	9	0.7
One bamboo staff	1	0	0.45
Two oak staffs	2	10	1.2
Seven reserve dog harnesses and two reserve hauling ropes	2	10	1.2
One coil of rope	0	6	0.18
Four bamboo poles for masts and for steering sledges	8	13	4.0
One bag of bread	5	15	2.7

One bag whey-powder	3	5	1.5
One bag sugar	2	3	1.0
One bag albuminous flour	1	12	0.8
One bag lime-juice tablets	1	10	0.73
One bag Frame-food stamina tablets	2	7	1.1
As boat's grips, under the sledges, were: Three sacks of pemmican (together)	238	1	108.2
One sack "leverpostei," or pâté made of calf's liver	93	15	42.7

SLEDGE NO. 2.

ON THIS WERE CARRIED, IN STRONG SACKS:	Lbs.	Oz.	Kilos.
Albuminous flour	14	15	6.8
Wheat flour	15	6	7.0
Whey-powder	16	15	7.7
Corn flour	8	13	4.0
Sugar	7	1	3.2
Vril-food	31	4	14.2
Australian pemmican	13	0	5.9
Chocolate	12	12	5.8
Oatmeal	11	0	5.0
Dried red whortleberries	0	14	0.4
Two sacks of white bread (together)	69	5	31.5
One sack of aleuronate bread	46	10	21.2
"Special food" (a mixture of pea flour, meat-powder, fat, etc.)	63	13	29.0
Butter	85	13	39.0
Fish flour (Våge's)	34	2	15.5
Dried potatoes	15	3	6.9
One reindeer-skin sleeping-bag	19	13	9.0
Two steel-wire ropes, with couples for twenty-eight dogs	11	0	5.0
One pair hickory snowshoes [skis]	11	0	5.0
Weight of sledge	43	5	19.7

SLEDGE NO. 3 (WITH JOHANSEN'S KAYAK)	Lbs.	Oz.	Kilos.
Kayak	41	6	18.8
Two pieces of reindeer-skin, to prevent chafing	1	12	0.8
A supply of dog-shoes	1	3	0.55
One Eskimo shooting-sledge with sail (intended for possible seal-shooting on the ice)	1	10	0.73
Two sledge sails	2	10	1.2
Pump	0	14	0.4
Oar-blades (made of canvas stretched on frames, and intended to be lashed to the ski-staffs)	1	2	0.5
Gun	7	2.7	3.26
Flask	0	5.9	0.17
Net (for catching crustacea in the sea)	0	5.2	0.15
One pair "komager"	1	15.7	0.9
Waterproof kayak overcoat of sealskin	2	3	1.0
Fur gaiters	0	7.3	0.21
Two reserve pieces of wood	0	9.8	0.28
Two tins of petroleum (about 5 gallons)	40	0.6	18.2
Several reserve snowshoe [ski] fastenings	0	15.1	0.43
Lantern for changing plates, etc.	1	1.2	0.49
Artificial glass horizon	0	10.2	0.29
Bag with cords and nautical almanac	0	4.6	0.13
Pocket sextant	0	13.7	0.39
Two packets of matches	0	13.7	0.39
One reserve sheet of German silver (for repaving plates under sledge-runners)	0	7.4	0.21

Pitch	0	3.5	0.1
Two minimum thermometers in cases	0	7.4	0.21
Three quicksilver thermometers in cases	0	4.9	0.14
One compass	0	8.8	0.25
One aluminium compass	0	8.4	0.24
One aluminium telescope	1	8.6	0.7
"Sennegraes" for Finn shoes	0	7	0.2
Bag with cartridges	26	1	11.85
Leather pouch with reserve shooting requisites, parts for gun-locks, reserve cocks, balls, powder, etc.	3	1	1.4
Leather pouch with glass bottle, one spoon, and five pencils	0	10.6	0.3
Bag with navigation tables, Nautical Almanack, cards, etc.	2	7	1.1
Tin box with diaries, letters, photographs, observation-journals, etc.	3	10	1.65
One cap for covering hole in deck of kayak	0	8	0.23
One sack of meat-chocolate	17	10	8.0
One bag of soups	6	10	3.0
One bag cocoa	7	6	3.35
One bag fish flour	3	12	1.70
One bag wheat flour	2	0	0.90
One bag chocolate	4	6	2.0
One bag oatmeal	4	6	2.0
One bag vril-food	4	6	2.0
As grips under the sledge were:			
One sack of oatmeal	29	1	13.2
One sack pemmican	115	1	52.3
One sack liver pâté	111	12	50.8

A List of Nansen's Dogs

on STARTING the TREK to the NORTH POLE

Dog Name	Lbs.	Kilos.
KVIK	78	35.7
FREIA	50	22.7
BARBARA	49 1/2	22.5
SUGGEN	61 1/2	28.0
FLINT	59 1/2	27.0
BARRABAS	61 1/2	28.0
GULEN	60 1/2	27.5
HAREN	61 1/2	28.0
BARNET	39	17.7
SULTAN	68	31.0
KLAPPERSLANGEN	59 1/2	27.0
BLOK	59	26.8
BJELKI	38	17.3
SJØLIGET	40	18.0
KATTA	45 1/2	20.7
NARRIFAS	46	21.0
LIVJÆGEREN	38 1/2	17.5
POTIFAR	57	26.0
STORRÆVEN	70	31.8
ISBJØN	61 1/2	28.0
LILLERÆVEN	59	26.7
KVINDFOLKET	37	26.0
PERPETUUM	63	28.6
BARO	60 1/2	27.5
RUSSEN	58	26.5
KAIFAS	69	31.5
ULENKA	57	26.0
PAN	65	29.5

Dogs near the Fram.

Dogs and Polar Exploration

*B*EFORE SNOW MACHINES arrived in the Arctic in the 1960s, sled dogs were used for travel and hauling supplies in inaccessible areas. Archaeological evidence shows that domestic dogs pulled sleds and helped in hunting as far back as nine thousand years ago in northeastern Siberia.

In the first days of polar exploration, sled dogs were used with mixed success. Dogsledding for polar travel required a lot of work. Walking or skiing beside the sled, which was heavy with gear and supplies, the musher had to guide the dogs over pressure ridges and around open water leads. For lack of experience, early attempts to use dogs for polar exploration were generally not successful. All who attempted to use them reverted to man-hauling. Nansen was the first successful polar explorer to use dogs on his North Pole journey.

Nansen's dogs were Ostiak dogs from northern Siberia, sometimes referred to as West Siberian Huskies, with perhaps a few Samoyeds thrown in. Nansen never refers to his dogs as huskies, so I have used the term sled dog to keep this simple and accurate. Kvik was the only dog Nansen brought from Norway. He collected thirty-four sled dogs from a friend, a Russian explorer who brought them to the northern shore of Siberia to go aboard the *Fram* because Nansen couldn't get them in Oslo before his expedition departed; a few were born on board the ship. The Asiatic Ostiak breed is used for sled hauling and elk, bear, and wolf hunting. Although comparatively small, these hardy dogs make good pullers.

North Pole Expeditions and Records

of FARTHEST NORTH

Inuit voyages in the far north. Earliest evidence of humans in the Arctic goes back 40,000 years.

330–32. BCE Greek navigator Pytheas from Marsallia (now Marseilles) travels from the Mediterranean to Britain and on to a place he called *Thule*, perhaps the Shetlands, Iceland, or Norway.

CE 986 Viking Erik the Red founds the first Norse settlements on Greenland.

1585–87 John Davis makes three voyages looking for a Northwest Passage (73°12′ N).

1594–97 William Barents (sometimes listed as Barentz) leads three voyages looking for a Northeast Passage (77°20′ N).

1607 Henry Hudson passes Spitsbergen, Norway, and records 80°23′ N as his farthest north point (likely it was 79°23′, or 637 nautical miles from the North Pole).

1806 Captain William Scoresby, whaler, is the first to sail into the Polar Sea (81°30′ N, or 510 miles from the pole).

1827 William Parry's Royal Navy Expedition is said to have arrived within 435 miles of the North Pole (82°45′ N).

1845–47 Sir John Franklin, Great Britain, searches for the Northwest Passage. Both of his boats are lost. They were found south of King William Sound—first the *Erebus*, in 2014, and then the *Terror*, in 2016.

1871 Charles Francis Hall, American, in the ship *Polaris*, travels via the Smith Sound route between Greenland and Ellesmere Island but dies during the winter on the pack ice (82°11′ N).

1872–74 The Austro-Hungarian North Pole Expedition in the *Tegetthoff*. With a crew of twenty-four, Captain Karl Weyprecht and Julius Payer left Tromsø, Norway, in July 1872. In August their ship was locked in ice and while drifting north, they discovered the archipelago they named Franz Josef Land after the Austro-Hungarian emperor. Payer took sleds out to explore and reached 81°50′ N. In May 1874, Captain Weyprecht and the expedition team abandoned the *Tegetthoff*, taking with them sleds and boats. They made it back to Vardø, Norway, on August 14, 1874.

1875–76 During the British Arctic Expedition led by Captain George Nares, Lieutenant Albert H. Markham traveled, by dogsled, from the ship HMS *Alert* on the north coast of Ellesmere Island and reached 83°20′ N, four hundred miles from the North Pole.

1878–79 The Swedish *Vega* Expedition, led by geologist Adolf Erik Nordenskiöld, attempted to discover the long-sought Northeast Passage. Nordenskiöld's maps and descriptions of the terrain would prove helpful to Nansen as the *Fram* moved through the waters above Siberia.

1879–81 USS *Jeannette* expedition with Lt. George Washington De Long (commander) and George W. Melville (chief engineer). Following the shipwreck of the *Jeannette*, De Long and eleven men died while others made their way to land and then to rescue.

1881 Benjamin Leigh Smith of Britain explored and charted parts of Franz Josef Land. He hoped to find De Long's ship, the *Jeannette*. When his ship was nipped by ice and crushed, he and his crew were forced to survive for ten months at Cape Flora on Northbrook Island. They finally headed south and were rescued.

1882 The Greely/Lady Franklin Bay Expedition, American, traveled by dogsled from the north coast of Ellesmere Island to 83°24′ N.

1888 First successful crossing of Greenland's inland ice by the Norwegian expedition led by Fridtjof Nansen (traveling from east to west).

1895 Fridtjof Nansen and Hjalmar Johansen, Norwegian, traveled by dogsled from the ship *Fram* around 84°N in the polar sea and returned to Franz Josef Land. They reached 86°14′N and 232 miles from the North Pole, and the farthest north to date by 174 nautical miles.

1897 The Swedish balloonist S. A. Andrée planned to take a hydrogen balloon from Spitsbergen directly over the pole to Russia or Canada. Andrée set off in July but crashed on the ice after only three days. His team survived the crash but died later on a small island. Their fate was unknown until the remains of their camp were found in 1930.

1900 Captain Umberto Cagni, Italian, of the Spanish Duke d'Abruzzi Expedition, traveled by dogsled from Franz Josef Land (86°34′N).

1906 Disputed (Considered questionable). Robert E. Peary, American, traveled by dogsled from the north coast of Ellesmere Island (87°6′N).

April 21, 1908. Disputed (unverifiable). Frederick A. Cook, American, traveled by dogsled from the northern tip of Axel Heiberg Island (90° N).

April 6, 1909. Disputed (unverifiable). Robert Peary and Matthew Henson traveled by dogsled, from the north coast of Ellesmere Island (90° N).

May 9, 1926. Disputed. Richard Byrd and pilot Floyd Bennett, in a Fokker F-VII Trimotor, the *Josephine Ford*, claim to be the first to fly over the pole.

May 12, 1926. Norwegian Roald Amundsen, American Lincoln Ellsworth, and Italian Umberto Nobile carry out the first transpolar flight from Spitsbergen to Alaska over the North Pole in the dirigible balloon *Norge*.

June 18–20, 1937. Soviet pilot Valery Chkalov carried out the first transpolar flight over the North Pole in an airplane, traveling from Moscow to Vancouver, Washington.

May 21, 1937. The first North Pole ice station was established by the Soviet Union at 89°25′N, twelve miles from the North Pole. Research was conducted for 274 days, after which the scientists were rescued by ice-breaker, having drifted 1,770 miles to the east coast of Greenland.

April 23, 1948. Twenty-four Soviet scientists and the flight crews from three planes became the first people to land, then stand on the North Pole.

May 9, 1949. Vitaly Volovich and Andrei Medvedev, of the Soviet Union, were the first to parachute onto the North Pole.

August 3, 1958. The nuclear-powered submarine USS *Nautilus* was the first naval vessel to reach the North Pole.

April 19, 1968. Ralph Plaisted was the first confirmed person to reach the North Pole; he traveled by Ski-doo (snow machine). Because both Peary's and Cook's claims to have reached the North Pole are in doubt, Plaisted's might be the first surface expedition to accomplish the feat.

April 6, 1969. Sir Walter "Wally" Herbert, Allan Gill, Dr. Roy Koerner, Dr. Ken Hedges, and forty dogs were the first to reach the North Pole by dogsled. They then traversed the Arctic Ocean. After setting out in 1968 from Barrow, Alaska, the expedition had been forced to winter near the pole due to ice drift and then continue on the following spring. They ended their trek in Spitsbergen, Norway.

August 17, 1977. The Soviet Union's nuclear-powered icebreaker *Arktika* was the first surface ship to reach the pole.

March 16–May 31, 1979. The members of the Dmitry Shparo Expedition, of the Soviet Union, were the first to ski from the continent to the North Pole.

March 7–May 1, 1986. The first expedition to reach the pole without resupply (one way) was the Steger International Polar Expedition. Team members: Will Steger, Paul Schurke, Brent Boddy, Richard Weber, Geoff Carroll, Ann Bancroft, Bob Mantell, Bob McKerrow, and five dog teams. Ann became the first woman to trek to the pole. The two Bobs and three dog teams returned to the base camp before the pole.

June 15, 1995. Canadian Richard Weber and Russian Dr. Mikhail Malakhov achieved the first round-trip journey to the pole using only human resources—no help, no dogs, no planes, no resupply. At 108 days, this was the longest unsupported North Pole journey.

2007 *Top Gear: Polar Special*, BBC's Top Gear team, are the first to reach the magnetic North Pole in a car.

A Special Note on Geoff Carroll

and A MODERN-DAY SLED DOG TRIP
to the NORTH POLE

*G*EOFF CARROLL, WHO lives in Barrow, Alaska, (recently changed to its traditional Iñupiaq name, Utqiaġvik), was an essential part of the 1986 Will Steger International Polar Expedition to the North Pole (the first confirmed dogsled journey to the North Pole without resupply). In addition to being a friend for years and talking to me about his life with dogs and raising a family in Barrow, Geoff shared with me his handwritten journal of those fifty-five days it took him and his companions to reach the North Pole. After two months of grueling travel over ice ridges and quick-freezing open water leads, Geoff reached the North Pole on May 1, 1986.

He told me, "First of all, we knew we weren't going to kill or eat our dogs, and we weren't going to feed dogs to dogs. To be the first sled dog trek with no resupply to the North Pole, one major concession was that a plane would meet us halfway up to take some dogs out. Same as Nansen, we just couldn't haul enough food for all the dogs and ourselves all the way to the pole. We started with forty-nine dogs, and roughly half were flown out along the way.

"Going out on a trip with sled dogs is like going out with your ten best friends. There's love there, but, even more than love, there's respect. Those guys are so tough. It's just amazing the weather they can survive and even be comfortable in. We certainly didn't baby the dogs. But they were a source of motivation and encouragement to the rest of us. They worked hard all day, and then they'd jump up the next morning full of enthusiasm to pull the sleds. Day after day. 'Come on, come on, let's go,' they seemed to say. It was such an inspiration. Sometimes we'd get down in the dumps and think, *What the heck are we doing here anyway?* But every day the dogs jumped up ready to go."

GOING TO THE BATHROOM
ON A TREK TO THE NORTH POLE

Geoff told me, "I don't know how Nansen did it, but it may have been similar to my experience. Number one was not much of an issue except for the old 'six inches of insulation and only three inches of anatomy' problem. I had to do a bit of stretching to make sure I didn't pee on the inside of my pants. We had pee bottles that we used when we were in the tents, which made life a lot easier.

"Number two was one of the most challenging activities of the expedition. It was one of the few things that required baring the hands.

My procedure was to strategically place four squares of TP in an easily accessible place in my clothing. Then I would run a short distance to build up my body heat while swinging my arms in circles to get as much warming blood into my fingertips as possible. When I felt I was ready, I would stop, take off my mittens, pull down my wind pants, open up the back hatch on my polar suit, and do my business as quickly as possible. I quickly grabbed my conveniently placed TP, cleaned things up, Velcroed up my back hatch, and pulled up my pants. Probably in the span of fifteen seconds. Even in that short time period, things got chilled, so I danced and waved my hands around until everything warmed up.

"It only happened once on the trip, but I did suffer the classic Arctic disaster. I went through my routine, quickly closed up my back hatch, and looked back to admire my work. There was nothing on the ice! That only left one place it could be, so I whipped my back hatch open, reached in and threw out the offensive object, and cleaned things up as best I could. That was not a good way to start the day.

"An interesting note was that the dogs loved eating human poop. They would go to great lengths to avoid stepping in dog poop, but they loved to eat human poop. If a dog driver running one of the teams ahead of you didn't move far enough off the trail when they pooped, my dogs would smell it and we'd nearly have a riot with the dogs trying to be the first one to get to it and eat it. When one of my dogs was not feeling well, I presented him with some poop on a piece of caribou skin. It really perked him up. This is probably more than you wanted to know."

Geoff told me why he took many solo trips after going to the North Pole.

"One of the great things about traveling across sea ice is that it is probably the most untouched wilderness in the world. Since most of it re-forms every year, it is totally pristine. I especially liked the times I would get separated from the other teams and I would be traveling in one of the most isolated places on earth with the dogs all in sync, in nearly absolute silence, the only sound being the padding of the dogs' feet, some panting, and a bit of squeaking from the sled. The dogs were content because they were doing their absolute favorite thing in the world. And so was I."

Geoff Carroll and his dog team giving kids rides during Spring Festival in Utqiaġvik (Barrow, Alaska).

Navigating in the Arctic

EXPLANATION *of* NAVIGATING *at the* NORTH POLE

by PAUL SCHURKE

(navigator on 1986 North Pole trek with Geoff Carroll)

*G*IVEN THE SHIFTING sea and extreme temperatures, virtually every process of adventuring is more challenging near the North Pole than elsewhere, except one: celestial navigation. First off, because the lines of longitude are converging toward a singularity at the top of the world, polar navigators can dispense with that element and simply focus on latitude, which makes the position-finding task far easier. Secondly, the sun keeps you on a northbound track. In the Arctic spring (prime time for polar travel) the sun is out round-the-clock and dips to its lowest point, due north, at local midnight and its highest point, due south, at local time.

The dip and rise are very subtle, so on our 1986 dogsled and ski expedition to the North Pole, here's how we'd find them: Within an hour of local noon (which we'd track with our watches), our team would stop for a rest break while I'd secure our sextant to the handles of a dogsled for stability. Then every few minutes, I'd scope the sun through the eyepiece and note its elevation on the instrument's graduated arc. As the sun approached peak position, its rise would "stall out" a bit, alerting me to take more precise and frequent sightings so that I could capture that exact reading at "zenith."

That sun-sighting process was painful in the deep cold, since it required delicate movements of bare fingers on cold brass dials. But the final step was easy: I'd refer to my navigational tables for the exact elevation of the sun at the North Pole during that moment of local noon. Then I'd subtract that figure from my sextant reading, and the remainder, in minutes of arc, equaled the number of nautical miles to our goal. My "celestial" reward upon reaching the North Pole was viewing a sun that remained exactly the same angle above the horizon every hour of night and day, cutting a perfect circle in the sky.

Simple Use of the Sun

and a 24-HOUR WATCH

by GEOFF CARROLL

ONE WAY TO find your way north is to use the sun and the time of day. At a time when the sun is always in the sky within hundreds of miles of the North Pole in spring and summer, at local solar noon, the sun is directly south, and at midnight it is north. So to head north, you head toward the sun at midnight and have it at your back at noon. Every hour in between is another 15° on your watch. So as you remain pointing north, the sun goes around you during the day. Therefore, if you keep your direction of travel properly oriented to the course of the sun, you are always pointed north. With a twenty-four-hour watch you can point the hour hand at the sun, and 0 will be pointing north.

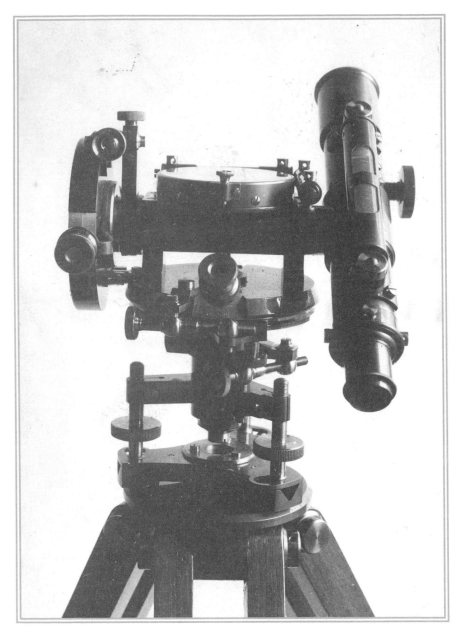

An instrument for observing the sun,
later used in the Arctic Expedition in the Arctic Ocean.

Time Line

October 10, 1861
Fridtjof Nansen born at Store Frøen, near Oslo.

1882
Volunteered on the sealer *Viking*. First saw Greenland's ice cap and was entranced by the Arctic world of sea ice. Decided to return someday.

1882–1888
Junior curator of zoology at the Bergen Museum.

1884
Trekked across Norway from Bergen to Oslo and back on skis.

1888
In April, defended his dissertation on the central nervous system of certain lower vertebrates and received a doctorate degree from the University of Oslo.

1888
Crossed Greenland in two months with a party of six, man-hauling all supplies (no dogs) from the uninhabited east coast to the towns on the west coast. They missed the boat back to Europe and remained with Inuit villagers through the winter.

1889
Nansen married Eva Sars.

1889–1892
Served as curator of the University of Oslo's Zootomical Institute. He published several articles and two books, *The First Crossing of Greenland* (1890) and *Eskimo Life* (1891).

1893–1896
Voyage of the *Fram*.
Locking his ship into the ice
above Siberia, Nansen and
his crew moved very slowly toward
the North Pole. When they
realized that the ship would not
reach the exact pole, Nansen
and Hjalmar Johansen supplied
themselves with thirty days' rations
for their dogs and a hundred days'
rations for themselves and set out
in March 1895. After getting closer
to the pole than anyone had before,
they traveled to Franz Josef Land,
wintered there, and started south
again in May 1896. They were
reunited with their crew in August
at Tromsø.

1897
Published *Farthest North: Being the
Record of a Voyage of Exploration of
the Ship "Fram" 1893–96 and of a
Fifteen Months' Sleigh Journey by
Dr. Nansen and Lieut. Johansen*.
Appointed a research professor at the
University of Oslo (at the time,
Kristiana). He also published six
volumes of scientific observations
made on the polar expedition.

1907
Nansen's wife, Eva, died of
pneumonia. Nansen became
a single father of five children.

1908
Appointed professor of oceanography at the University of Oslo.

1905–1908
Promoting the independence of
Norway from Sweden, he served as
Norway's minister to Great Britain.

1914
At the beginning of World War I,
Nansen became more and more
involved in international politics.

1917–1918
Led a Norwegian delegation in
Washington, DC, and negotiated an
agreement to ease the Allied
blockade so that shipments of
essential food could proceed.

1919
Became president of the Norwegian
Union for the League of Nations
and was an influential presence at
the Peace Conference in Paris.

1919

Nansen married Sigrun Munthe.

1920

Began his long service as a delegate to the League of Nations. When asked by the League to take on the job of repatriating the prisoners of war, Nansen helped repatriate 450,000 prisoners.

1921

Appointed High Commissioner for Refugees. Nansen invented the Nansen Passport, a document of identification issued to stateless refugees, which was recognized by fifty-two nations.

1921

Nansen led a European relief effort, through organizations like the Red Cross and Save the Children, to aid the millions of Russians dying in the famine of 1921–22, while Herbert Hoover led the American relief operation.

1922

Following a conflict between Turkey and Greece, Nansen negotiated the resettlement of about 1.25 million Greeks living on Turkish soil back to their homeland, while as many as five hundred thousand Turks moved from land controlled by Greece.

1922

Nansen was awarded the Nobel Peace Prize.

1925

Nansen headed a League of Nations delegation to determine whether fifty thousand Armenian refugees could be settled in Soviet Armenia. They had the opportunity to have Nansen Passports, and so were protected as refugees under his High Commissioner's office.

May 13, 1930

Died at sixty-eight years old.

May 17, 1930

Buried on Norway's Constitution Day.

Digging the Fram *out of the ice.*

Glossary

THE ARCTIC: The word comes from the Greek *arktikos*, meaning "near the bear," and refers to the constellation known as Ursa Major, or the Big Dipper. (The two stars on the end of the Big Dipper point to Polaris, or the North Star.) The Arctic is the polar region north of the Arctic Circle. During the June solstice, there are twenty-four hours of sunlight in the Arctic and on the December solstice, the sun never rises. The Arctic includes eight countries: Finland, Sweden, Norway, Iceland, Greenland (under the Danish monarchy), Canada, the United States (Alaska), and Russia. Temperatures in the Arctic range from −40°C (−40°F) in the winter to 10°C (50°F), in the summer.

ARCTIC CIRCLE: The Arctic Circle is a parallel of latitude (about 66°33′ N. latitude), 1,650 miles (2,655 km) from the North Pole. The Arctic Circle does not actually enclose all the Arctic regions.

ARCTIC ICE PACK OR PACK ICE: The ice cover of the Arctic Ocean. The ice melts in spring and summer. After reaching its minimum around mid-September, it increases during the fall and winter. Some ice survives through the year, but with changes in global temperatures, there has been a dramatic decline of ice in the Arctic in recent decades.

CROW'S NEST: A structure in the upper part of the mast of a ship that is used as a lookout point.

FRAM: The 128-foot ship built by shipwright Colin Archer for Fridtjof Nansen's Arctic expedition. It was designed to freeze into the Arctic ice pack so the explorers could "float" over the North Pole. (The word *Fram* means "forward" in Norwegian.) Later the ship was used for Arctic and Antarctic expeditions by Otto Sverdrup and Roald Amundsen. The *Fram* traveled farther north (85°57′N) and farther south (78°41′S) than any other wooden ship and is preserved at the *Fram* Museum in Oslo, Norway.

FROSTBITE: Damage to skin caused by extreme cold. Fingers, toes, and noses are most often affected.

GREENLAND: A territory controlled by Denmark that lies between the Arctic and Atlantic Oceans. It is the largest island in the world. Three-quarters of Greenland is permanent ice, and even today it is the least densely populated country in the world. Inhabited by native peoples from Canada for five thousand years, Greenland's south and west coasts received settlers from Norway, Iceland, and Denmark in the tenth century.

HUMMOCK: A low hill of broken ice that has been forced upward by pressure. It may be fresh or weathered.

ICELAND: A Nordic island country in the North Atlantic.

ICE BLINK: A white glare seen on the underside of low clouds indicating the presence of ice, which may be beyond the range of vision or over the horizon.

ICE CAP: A permanent sheet of ice that covers land or water.

ICE FLOE: A large flat sheet of floating ice, meters or more across. A giant floe might be over 5.4 nautical miles across.

ICE PAN: A large contiguous section of floating pack ice. These are always in flux. Sometimes they add ice and get bigger. Sometimes they break up into smaller pans.

JEANNETTE CURRENT: Nansen postulated that a northeasterly current would take the *Fram* from the New Siberian Islands off the coast of Russia up and over or near the North Pole and deposit the ship somewhere on the other side of the globe between Greenland and Spitsbergen. He called it the "Jeannette" current because of the debris from the shipwrecked *Jeannette*, which was crushed near the New Siberian Islands and washed up on the coast of Greenland a few years later.

KOMAGER: A Sami moccasin/boot for use in less cold Arctic months.

LATITUDE: A measure of relative position north or south on the Earth's surface, measured in degrees from the equator, which has a latitude of 0°, with the poles each having a latitude of 90° north or south. The distance of a degree of latitude is about 69 statute miles or 60 nautical miles (111 km).

LEAD: A fracture or passageway through ice which is navigable by surface vessels. Freshly refrozen leads are often covered with dark ice and are among the most dangerous things polar explorers encounter. In cold temperatures, ice in the leads gets thicker and provides smooth routes through rough ice sections.

LONGITUDE: Lines of longitude run between the North Pole and the South Pole. They are a certain distance apart at the equator but get closer together as they go north (and south). These lines are also called meridians. Like lines of latitude, meridians are measured in degrees, minutes, and seconds. The north-south line that marks 0° longitude passes through Greenwich, England. This is called the Greenwich, or prime, meridian.

MIDNIGHT SUN: The sun visible through the night in the summer months north of the Arctic Circle and south of the Antarctic Circle. In the Arctic during the summer solstice, June 21, the sun is visible for a full twenty-four hours.

NAUTICAL MILE: A unit in measuring distances at sea or on ice, equal to one minute of latitude, approximately 2,025 yards (1,852 m), as opposed to a statute mile, which is a unit for measuring land distances.

NIPPED: Beset in the ice with the surrounding ice forcibly pressing against the hull.

NORTHEAST PASSAGE: From the point of view of Europe, this is the shipping route to the Pacific Ocean from the northern Atlantic along the coasts of the Arctic Ocean, from Norway to Russia.

NORTHWEST PASSAGE: From the European viewpoint, the sea route to the Pacific Ocean through the Arctic Ocean along the northern coast of North America via waterways through the Canadian Arctic Archipelago.

NORTH POLE: The northernmost place on earth, located in the Arctic Ocean.

OLD ICE: Sea ice that has survived at least one summer's melt. Most topographic features on old ice are smoother than on first-year ice.

PEMMICAN: A high-energy food of concentrated protein—usually dried meat—and fat adopted by Europeans in the fur trade and later by polar explorers.

POLAR DAY AND NIGHT: The polar day occurs in the northernmost and southernmost regions of the earth when the sun stays above the horizon for more than twenty-four hours. The opposite phenomenon, polar night, occurs when the night lasts for more than twenty-four hours.

PRESSURE RIDGES: When ice pans crush into one another, the ice along the edges breaks up and gets pushed up into pressure ridges. These can range from very small to up to 50 feet (15 m) tall. When ice pans freeze together into one larger pan, the large pan can have pressure ridges crisscrossing it. Some pressure ridges are made up of recently broken-up ice and some are more rounded and weathered.

SAMI PEOPLE: An indigenous Arctic people, formerly known as Lapps or Laplanders, who live in the far north of Scandinavia and Russia.

SCURVY: A debilitating illness characterized by swollen gums and extremities, a yellowing of the skin, and pain in the joints. Untreated, it leads to death. It is caused by a lack of Vitamin C (found in fresh fruits and vegetables) in the diet over a prolonged time.

SEXTANT: A precision instrument that includes a telescope and is used to measure the elevation of celestial bodies (planets and stars) above the horizon to determine one's position.

SPITSBERGEN: The largest island of the Svalbard archipelago in northern Norway, which was used as a whaling outpost in the seventeenth century.

STATUTE MILE: A unit of measure on land equal to 1,760 yards (1,609 m). As opposed to a nautical mile, which is a unit to measure distances at sea or on ice.

SUET: The hard fat around a cow's or sheep's kidneys, which can be melted and used for food or other purposes.

SVALBARD: A Norwegian archipelago in the Arctic Ocean, known prior to 1925 by its Dutch name Spitsbergen, meaning "jagged mountains."

TRACES: Straps, usually leather, that connect sled dogs to one another and to the sled, allowing them to pull it.

WALRUS BLUBBER: The fat layer on a walrus that serves as both food and fuel for the people of the north.

WATER SKY: The dark streaks on the undersides of low clouds, indicating the presence of open water in the vicinity of sea ice. The dark clouds over open water have long been used by polar explorers and scientists to navigate in sea ice.

Sources

*D*OCUMENTED AND RESEARCHED with primary and secondary sources, including documents from the Fridtjof Nansen Archives at the National Library of Norway and the following conversations and some taped interviews with Harald Dag Jølle of the Norwegian Polar Institute, in Tromsø; Karen Blaauw Helle, emeritus professor of physiology, the Department of Biomedicine, University of Bergen, Bergen, Norway; Carl Emil Vogt, University of Oslo and the Center for Studies of Holocaust and Religious Minorities; Susan Barr, senior polar adviser, Riksantikvaren/ Directorate for Cultural Heritage; Anne Melgård at the National Library of Norway in Oslo; Karin Berg, former director Oslo's Holmenkollen Ski Museum; Geir O. Kløver, director, *Fram* Museum; Tom Nickelsen Gram, tour guide at the *Fram* Museum; Ola Just Haugbo, manager of information systems, Fridtjof Nansen Institute; Paul Schurke, Craig George, Gerald Johnson, Geoff Carroll, Joanne Muratori, and Will Ambrose, vice-dean for the School of the Coastal Environment at Coastal Carolina University.

Selected Bibliography
and Resources

Bain, J. Arthur. *Life and Explorations of Fridtjof Nansen.* (reprint of 1897 book)
London: Forgotten Books, 2017.

Hall, Anna. *Nansen.* New York: Viking Press, 1940.

Helle, Karen B., and Ortwin Bock. *Fridtjof Nansen and the Neuron.* Bergen,
Norway: Bodoni Forlag, 2016.

Huntford, Roland. *Nansen: The Explorer as Hero.* London: Abacus, 2001.

Jackson, Frederick G. *A Thousand Days in the Arctic,* Volumes 1 and 2.
London: Harper & Brothers, 1899.

Jacobs, Francine. *A Passion for Danger: Nansen's Arctic Adventures.* New York:
Putnam, 1994.

Johansen, Hjalmar. *With Nansen in the North: A Record of the* Fram *Expedition in
1893–96.* Cambridge, UK: Cambridge University Press, 1899, 2012.

Johnson, Charles W. *Ice Ship: The Epic Voyages of the Polar Adventurer* Fram.
Lebanon, NH: ForeEdge, 2014.

Nansen, Fridtjof. *Farthest North: Being a Record of Exploration of the ship "Fram"*
1893–96 and of a Fifteen Months' Sleigh Journey by Dr. Nansen and Lieut.
Johansen, Volumes 1 and 2. New York: Harper & Brothers, 1897.

———*Sporting Days in Wild Norway: Passages from My Diary*. London:
T. Butterworth, Ltd., 1st Ed. 1925.

Nansen, Fridtjof, and Hubert Majendie Gepp (trans.). *The First Crossing of*
Greenland. London: Longmans, Green, and Co., 1890.

Nansen, Fridtjof, and William Archer (trans.). *Eskimo Life*. London: Longman,
Green, and Co., 1893.

Scott, J. M. *Fridtjof Nansen*. London: Heron, 1971.

Sides, Hampton. *In the Kingdom of Ice: The Grand and Terrible Polar Voyage*
of the USS Jeannette. New York: Doubleday, 2014.

———"1,000 Days in the Ice." *National Geographic*, Jan. 2009.

Sverdrup, Otto, and T. C. Fairley. *Sverdrup's Arctic Adventures*. London: Longman,
Green, Co., 1959.

Wallace, Sandra Neil, and Rich Wallace. *Bound by Ice: A True North Pole Survival*
Story. Honesdale, Pennsylvania: Calkins Creek, 2017.

Websites

FRAM MUSEUM, Oslo, Norway
FRAMMUSEUM.NO

THE NANSEN COLLECTION
COMMONS.WIKIMEDIA.ORG/WIKI/CATEGORY:THE_NANSEN_COLLECTION

THE NATIONAL LIBRARY OF NORWAY/ARCHIVE OF FRIDTJOF NANSEN
NB.NO/EN/THE-NATIONAL-LIBRARY-OF-NORWAY/

NOBELPRIZE.ORG
NOBELPRIZE.ORG/NOBEL_PRIZES/PEACE/LAUREATES/1922/NANSEN-BIO.HTML

NORWEGIAN POLAR INSTITUTE, Tromsø, Norway
NPOLAR.NO/EN/

SMITHSONIAN NATIONAL MUSEUM ARCTIC STUDIES CENTER
NATURALHISTORY.SI.EDU/ARCTIC/INDEX.HTML

PMEL (PACIFIC MARINE ENVIRONMENTAL LABORATORY) ARCTIC ZONE
National Oceanic and Atmospheric Administration
and United States Department of Commerce
PMEL.NOAA.GOV/ARCTIC-ZONE/ARCTIC-INFO.HTML

ALL ABOUT SEA ICE
National Snow and Ice Data Center
NSIDC.ORG/CRYOSPHERE/SEAICE/INDEX.HTML

Image Credits

p. vi, vii, 228, 229: From *Farthest North* by Dr. Fridtjof Nansen: Harper & Brothers Publishers, New York and London, 1897; p. xvi, xviii, 11, 14, 37, 54, 55 (top), 63 (bottom), 69, 77, 79, 82, 93, 112 (top), 130, 131, 143, 159, 168, 170, 183, 188, 202, 235, 243, 259 (middle), 260 (top), 260 (bottom), 261 (top), 261 (middle), 262 (middle), 262 (bottom): Fridtjof Nansen, Archives of Fridtjof Nansen, courtesy of the National Library of Norway; p. xix, 5, 6, 12 (top), 15, 17, 18 (top), 26, 27, 28, 29, 31, 39, 40, 41, 42, 44 (top), 44 (bottom), 45, 46, 47 (top), 49, 50, 51 (top), 51 (bottom), 52, 53, 56, 57 (top) 57 (bottom), 58 (top), 58 (bottom), 60, 61, 62, 63 (top), 64, 65, 66, 67, 68, 70, 72, 76, 81, 84, 88, 90, 91, 95, 98, 101, 107, 108, 109, 121, 122, 136, 137, 148, 155, 172, 176, 189 (top), 189 (bottom), 191, 192, 194, 209, 210, 218, 224, 225, 227, 230, 232, 234, 239, 241 (top), 242, 245, 247 (bottom), 254, 256, 262 (top), 263, 266, 267, 269, 278, 296: Archives of Fridtjof Nansen, courtesy of the National Library of Norway; p. 2 (top): Olsen and Thomsen, Archives of Fridtjof Nansen, courtesy of the National Library of Norway; p. 2 (middle): Adolf Christian Moestue, Archives of Fridtjof Nansen, courtesy of the National Library of Norway; p. 2 (bottom), 4, 12 (bottom), 18 (bottom), 19 (right), 237: (Ludwik Szaciński, Archives of Fridtjof Nansen, courtesy of the National Library of Norway; p. 7: From an 1882 photograph, Archives of Fridtjof Nansen, courtesy of the National Library of Norway; p. 8: C. Angerer and Göschl, Archives of Fridtjof Nansen, courtesy of the National Library of Norway; p. 9 (top), 34: Johan von der Fehr, Archives of Fridtjof Nansen, courtesy of the National Library of Norway; p. 9 (bottom): H. Abels Kunstforlag, Archives of Fridtjof Nansen, courtesy of the National Library of Norway; p. 13: Johan Lund, Archives of Fridtjof Nansen, courtesy of the National Library of Norway; p. 19

(left): Joseph John Elliott and Clarence Edmund Fry, Archives of Fridtjof Nansen, courtesy of the National Library of Norway; p. 21: Wikimedia Commons, Gerardus Mercator, circa 1600; p. 25, 276: Map by Knud Larsen Bergslien, courtesy of the National Library of Norway; p. 38, 43, 59, 118, 223: Photo: Peter Lourie; p. 47 (bottom), 55 (bottom), 80, 86, 132, 259 (top), 259 (bottom), 260 (middle), 261 (bottom): Sigurd Scott-Hansen, Archives of Fridtjof Nansen, courtesy of the National Library of Norway; p. 48: H. Egidius and Fridtjof Nansen. Archives of Fridtjof Nansen, courtesy of the National Library of Norway; p. 71: Photo: Ellit and Fry, Archives of Fridtjof Nansen, courtesy of the National Library of Norway; p. 83: A. Bloch, Archives of Fridtjof Nansen, courtesy of the National Library of Norway; p. 96, 103, 112 (bottom), 114, 147, 152, 178, 181: From *Farthest North* by Dr. Fridtjof Nansen, Vol 2: Harper & Brothers Publishers, New York and London, 1897; p. 105, 117: A drawing by H. Egidius, from a photograph, in *Farthest North* by Dr. Fridtjof Nansen, Vol 2: Harper & Brothers Publishers, New York and London, 1897; p. 116: A drawing by A. Eiebakke, from a photograph, in *Farthest North* by Dr. Fridtjof Nansen, Vol. 2: Harper & Brothers Publishers, New York and London, 1897; p. 120, 126, 133, 140, 145, 198: A drawing by H Egidius in *Farthest North* by Dr. Fridtjof Nansen Vol 2: Harper & Brothers Publishers, New York and London, 1897; p. 123: Photo: Peter Lourie, *Fram* Museum, Oslo, Norway; p. 146: A drawing by Lars Jorde, from a photograph, in *Farthest North* by Dr. Fridtjof Nansen, Vol 2: Harper & Brothers Publishers, New York and London, 1897; p. 149, 173: Courtesy of the National Library of Norway; p. 158: A drawing by Otto Sinding, from *Farthest North* by Dr. Fridtjof Nansen, Vol 2: Harper & Brothers Publishers, New York and London, 1897; p. 164: Artist Lars Jorde depiction from a photograph, Archives of Fridtjof Nansen, courtesy of the National Library of Norway; p. 182: Frederik Hjalmar Johansen, Archives of Fridtjof Nansen, courtesy of the National Library of Norway; p. 195: Drawing by A. Bloch, from *Farthest North* by Dr. Fridtjof Nansen, Vol 2: Harper & Brothers Publishers, New York and London, 1897; p. 197: Drawing from *Farthest North* by Dr. Fridtjof Nansen, Vol 2: Harper & Brothers Publishers, New York and London, 1897; p. 203, 207, 208, 212, 215: F. Jackson, Archives of Fridtjof Nansen, courtesy of the National Library of Norway; p. 238: Taken from this scientific report, plate xx in part v of volume 1: scientific results: *The Norwegian North Polar Expedition 1893–1896: Vol. 1: [1–5]* Christiania: Dybwad, 1900–1906; p. 233: Anna Bielke, Archives of Fridtjof Nansen, courtesy of the National Library of Norway; p. 236: J. Wickstrøm, Archives of Fridtjof Nansen, courtesy of the National Library of Norway; p. 240: Harris and Ewing, Archives of Fridtjof Nansen, courtesy of the National Library of Norway; p. 241 (bottom): UNHCR, Archives of Fridtjof Nansen, courtesy of the National Library of Norway; p. 244: Ingeborg Motzfeldt Løchen, Archives of Fridtjof Nansen, courtesy of the National Library of Norway; p. 246, 265: Anders Beer Wilse, Archives of Fridtjof Nansen, courtesy of the National Library of Norway; p. 247 (top): Henriksen and Steen, Archives of Fridtjof Nansen, courtesy of the National Library of Norway; p. 248: Minjatjur, Archives of Fridtjof Nansen, courtesy of the National Library of Norway; p. 252: Fridtjof Nansen's print from a hand-colored photograph, Archives of Fridtjof Nansen, courtesy of the National Library of Norway; p. 288: Craig George; p. 292: H. Porter, Archives of Fridtjof Nansen, courtesy of the National Library of Norway

Index